THE

Yes

J O U R N E Y

A STORY OF STARTING WHERE YOU ARE
AND LIVING YOUR PURPOSE

Bill and Michele Heintz as told to Julie Larocco

Funds generated from sales of this book support The Foundry Ministries, Inc., a Christ-centered organization, which demonstrates remarkable success in restoring the lives of men and women battling life-dominating addictions. Learn more about these life-changing services at www.foundryministries.com.

For further information please contact Foundry Way Press by visiting TheYesJourney.org, FoundryMinistries.com, connect@theyesjourney.org or write to our offices.
Foundry Way Press
P.O. Box 824
Bessemer, AL 35021

Manufactured in the United States of America

Editor and Publisher: Larisa Lambert Mills
Cover Design by Miles Parsons and Larisa Lambert Mills
Cover Art by Betty K. Freeman
Interior Book Design by Bob Weathers

Copyedited by Julie Larocco, Drew Young and Iris Jones Mills

Printed by Deep South Printing, LLC

Covered in prayer by The Foundry Ministries Family

Library of Congress Control Number: 2016936851

Heintz, Bill and Michele as told to Larocco, Julie
The yes journey: a story of starting where you are and living your purpose.

ISBN: 978-0-9827104-2-5

THE

Yes

JOURNEY

Contents

Your YES Journey 1

That Moment 4

My Promised Land 8

A Path to Nowhere.. 15

A Path to Purpose 23

A Wave Goodbye.. 27

Leaving It All Behind... 32

Just Say "YES"... 35

The Trouble with YES 42

Shattered.. 48

YES with Conviction 54

Forgiveness 60

Detour to Decatur 69

Ministers and Partners 80

Trust on the Road 88

Giants in the Land 95

Rounding the Bend to the Promised Land........................ 101

Potholes in the Road ... Again!... 108

Promised Land or Bust!.. 114

I'm Not Going Anywhere 123

Endure, Wait and Trust... 129

Choosing to Change 133

Bigger Vision 145

Big Changes 151

The Long Haul.. 159

Living from the Promised Land 166

Share Your YES Journey 170

The YES Journey Daily Steps 171

The YES Journey Study Guide... 177

Your YES Journey

Dear Reader:

It's nearly impossible to sum up a lifetime of ministry with Bill in a few pages: the conception—the years of dreaming and planning about The Foundry—the birth of the ministry, the everyday work we are called to, so rich with memories of God's provision, grace, protection and faithfulness.

Naivety and inexperience can be a blessing when blazing a new trail. We had zeal, but had we known all the difficulties, challenges and major bumps in the road, we may have thrown in the proverbial towel. Our five amazing children also made many sacrifices as a result of our many flaws and for the sake of our ministry. I'm so grateful God didn't give us too many sneak previews of the things to be overcome and work to be done in both our private and public ministry lives. Instead, in his infinite wisdom, he gave us the grace needed for each step of the journey.

We have always found comfort knowing this is God's ministry. He has faithfully provided the direction, people and tools to build the programs. It is our hope that as Bill shares our story, and I add my perspective here and there, that it will bless, strengthen and encourage you through every step, pothole,

detour, question and triumph of your YES Journey and to your own personal Promised Land—whatever that may be.

Since we are sharing our YES Journey with you, it would mean a lot to us for you to share your YES Journey story with us at TheYESJourney.org. Please let us know what verses, thoughts, struggles and wisdom help you along the way, and where you are on your YES Journey.

To His Glory,

Michele Heintz

"Your Promised Land is the place
where God's personalized promises over
  your life
become a living reality
rather than a theological theory."

Beth Moore, "Believing God"

THAT Moment

A defining moment.

I call it a "THAT moment."

It's a point in time when a word, an action, a circumstance knocks you in the head and heart, and directs your steps toward a lifelong calling. A defining moment might tell you something you need to know about yourself. It might tell you to stop what you are doing and start something new. It can scare or exhilarate you—maybe both at the same time. And if it really is a "THAT moment," then you know it is the voice of God.

God has spoken to me many times and in many ways, but I can point to several defining moments that put me on a purposeful path toward the building of The Foundry Ministries. For instance, God used a cattle truck, a guy in a gutter and an ocean wave off Pompano Beach to show me things I needed to know about myself, and about his intentions for my life.

Though each of these experiences was pivotal for me, it was only in hindsight that I really recognized their significance; that through them, God was teaching me his will, his wisdom and his way for the journey toward my personal Promised Land.

4

My hope is that this book shows you that God is speaking to you through defining moments in your own life. **He has made you to be somebody—somebody with the purpose, passion and potential to enter a Promised Land of your own.** He has created you to be who he wants you to be, and he will give you the confidence to do what he has created you to do. All you have to do is say, "YES, Lord" when you hear his call.

God is trustworthy and he will continue to be so as he leads you to your Promised Land.

This will be the greatest journey of your life. I Peter 1:18-21 (The Message) says:

> **Your life is a journey you must travel with a deep consciousness of God. It cost God plenty to get you out of that dead-end, empty-headed life you grew up in. He paid with Christ's sacred blood, you know. He died like an unblemished, sacrificial lamb.**
>
> **And this was no afterthought. Even though it has only lately—at the end of the ages—become public knowledge, God always knew he was going to do this for you. It's because of this sacrificed Messiah, whom God then raised from the dead and glorified,**

5

that you trust God, that you know you have a future in God.

God always knew he was going to do this for you!

And for that reason, you can know with confidence you have a future in him. He may kick you out of the familiar. Let him. Having unshakable confidence in God will allow you to get out of whatever box you've gotten yourself into; give up what you haven't been willing to give up; and do what you never thought you could do.

Are you ready to find your Promised Land? If you are, let's get started! God will take you places you never dreamed you could go.

"Each of us—

whether black, brown, yellow, red, or white—

was conceived by destiny, produced by purpose and

packaged with potential to

live a meaningful, fulfilling life."

Dr. Myles Munroe, "Devotional & Journal"

My Promised Land

"Once upon a time, there was this messed up, ordinary guy…"

That's how I want to start this story, because for all the folks who say, "Look what you did, Bill!" and for all the folks who say, "Bill Heintz made The Foundry what it is today," I must respond with: "I didn't do it. I couldn't have."

The Foundry Ministries—this Promised Land of mine—was envisioned by God. Amazingly, God entrusted that vision to me and a whole lot of other brothers and sisters in Christ who stepped up to make it what it is today.

Every day I get to go to work at The Foundry. Because I love what I do so much, it's not work at all to me. It's an opportunity to do what I want to do, feel what I want to feel, accomplish what I want to accomplish. Can you imagine?

In this Promised Land of mine, I get to help people change their lives.

I get to help them have a happy ending.

In Jeremiah 29:11 (NIV), God assures his people with these words: "I

know the plans I have for you," declares the Lord, "plans to prosper you and not to harm you, plans to give you hope and a future." I get to help men and women recognize themselves as people for whom God created a future and a hope. And it sure feels good to be the messenger. You cannot imagine the joy I get playing a small part in the lives of once-hopeless people who are experiencing life-changing hope in Jesus Christ. They are reuniting with their parents, their wives, their husbands and their children. They are realizing their real potential and actively working toward better ways of life.

The Foundry Ministries is where all this joy happens. At first, that might not be evident to the man or woman who has come to us for help. For each one, in those first hours and days, The Foundry is a trauma center, an ICU, an emergency room. The people who come here believe they are so far gone that if something does not change right away, their lives will end up in torment and even death. Sadly, many of them are right.

The Foundry is God's cocoon for hurting people. People crawl in, hauling with them their messed up pasts, their shame and their self-inflicted bruises and cuts. Often they bring pain from abuse, neglect and life circumstances that are hard to bear. Some are so ashamed of what they have done under the influence of drugs and alcohol that their self-esteem is in the cellar. They are desperately aware of the hurts they have caused and just as desperate for forgiveness.

THE JOURNEY

But if they pay attention as they work through The Foundry's programs—listening for "THAT moments" God speaks into their lives—they find freedom in Jesus. They realize God loves them and forgives them. They become open to finding out who they are in Christ. They find out they have purpose and potential, and they look at their futures in a whole new way.

Something magnificent occurs and the beleaguered caterpillar that crawled into that cocoon turns into a beautiful butterfly and learns to fly.

This is what happened for me when I gave my life to Christ, so I know it's real, and I'm grateful for every day I can share it with someone else.

I made a mess of my life. I didn't like myself. I had no self-esteem to speak of. If you'd looked in the 1970s *Webster's Dictionary*, under the word "lazy," you would have found a picture of me. But Jesus Christ helped me break down the barriers I'd constructed through my addiction, laziness and selfishness. He showed me there is life after failure; there is freedom and forgiveness; and I didn't have to beat myself up any longer.

God delivered me from the torments of my past and introduced me to his grace. He showed me a new tomorrow. That's the miracle I get to share with others. That's the reason I come to work with a glad heart every day.

Some men and women come to The Foundry because a judge gave them an ultimatum, forcing them to choose between our program or prison. Some come to satisfy their families. Some come hating God. Some come with a really bad attitude. But one thing is true of all of them: no matter how hard they try, they can't hide from themselves.

Through Jesus Christ, we offer them a solution to their brokenness. We also address the side effects of addiction: a lack of willingness to be responsible or accountable for their lives. The Foundry is a safe place to heal, learn self-discipline, accept and work under authority, and make an effort to be a better person today than you were the day before.

I know this from my own experience: when you realize you are a new creation in Christ and tomorrow can look very different and so much better than the past, you gain self-respect and self-confidence. You don't want to hide from yourself. You can look in the mirror and like what you see.

I wasted many years walking outside of God's purpose for my life— doing my own thing. I was one of those guys who didn't like what I saw in the mirror. But today my life in this Promised Land is glorious! God took what I had to give and gave me more than I could ever dream of.

The Foundry Ministries is *my* Promised Land, yes, but **your Promised Land will look very different because it will include God's unique plan for *you*!** When you tap into God's vision for your life, when you allow

him to plant that seed in your life, you'll experience the excitement of watching that seed sprout, bud and grow. Then one day, you'll wake up and find it blossoming. You'll have a feeling of completeness and wholeness that you've never known before.

So what does your Promised Land look like? (To see what my Promised Land, The Foundry Ministries, looks like, go to www.foundryministries. com.) Mine is greater than I could have comprehended. Maybe God is calling you to be a minister like me. Or it could be something very different:

- a painter who makes things bright and beautiful

- a teacher who is gifted at helping people discover and build their skills

- a mother who raises her children to be compassionate and successful adults

- a writer, an entrepreneur, a farmer, a traveler.

Your Promised Land may be the day you realize you've overcome your addiction to drugs or alcohol or pornography or gambling or eating.

Your Promised Land could be the moment you decide to leave a codependent relationship and discover the joy of a relationship and life with Christ.

No matter what or where your Promised Land is, you will know it when you arrive. You will recognize that you've achieved a vision God has given just to you.

The day you step into your personal Promised Land, fulfilling the vision of what God has called you to be, you'll know without a doubt that you didn't do it on your own. You'll say, "I didn't do it. I couldn't have. All I did was say, 'YES, Lord.'"

"The two most important days of your life are the day you were born and the day you discover why you were born."

Mark Twain

A Path to Nowhere

My dad and mom attempted to instill in me a good work ethic and other disciplines I would need to become a man of integrity and worth. But somehow, I just didn't get the message.

In 1966, I decided to join the Army. I was 20 years old and knew it was just a matter of time before I was called up for the draft. By joining voluntarily, I had a better chance of choosing where I'd be stationed and what I'd be doing. After I got out of boot camp, I was stationed in Miami where I worked on a missile base every other day, 24 hours on and 24 hours off. I spent my days off at the beach with my buddies.

This was the life! The military was a cinch. I enjoyed myself so much I reenlisted, thinking I might make the Army a career. A year after I shipped out to a base in Furth, Germany, I returned to the States on a furlough, just long enough to marry a girl I'd dated a few times. She'd told me about the mental abuse she was suffering at home, and I decided it was up to me to rescue her.

In Germany, I worked in the finance division. It wasn't a difficult job, and I continued to enjoy the camaraderie that went with military life. But in 1969, a high-speed accident on the German Autobahn changed everything.

That accident almost took my life. In fact, I came near death three times during the medical treatment immediately following the accident. Then, after a blood clot formed in one of my lungs, I was flown back to the States where I spent the next several months in a full body cast at a medical facility at Fort Knox, Kentucky. In the meantime, my right femur had not healed properly and, when the body cast came off, one leg was a quarter inch shorter than the other. A shoe lift became a daily part of my wardrobe.

Soon after my honorable discharge in 1971, my wife and I divorced. I was 25 years old, but felt I'd already experienced a lifetime of hurt, so when a friend invited me to church, I agreed to go. After the service, the pastor prayed that God would heal my leg. Miraculously, it grew out right before my eyes and was restored to its original length—I no longer needed to wear the shoe lift!

Strangely, this was not a defining moment for me. Yes, I had a lot of questions about God, and it was obvious he was trying to get my attention, but somehow I just didn't get the message that he had a plan for my life.

I married again. This time to a girl I'd gone out with a few times—a rebound relationship following my divorce. We moved to an apartment complex in Louisville, Kentucky, and there I made the most destructive decision of my life. I'd made friends with a guy who lived in the apartment

building next to ours, and we began hanging out together. I didn't realize he was a drug user until the night he offered me a joint.

Now for years, I'd managed to avoid the endless stream of alcohol and drugs that were so readily available in the military, but that night the temptation to cope with my increasingly painful life with a little marijuana was more than I could resist. Within a few weeks, I was smoking pot regularly, then downing Quaaludes, and finally, ingesting any pill I could get my hands on that would get me high and keep me high.

I was married to a wonderful woman, and we had a newborn daughter, but my increasing addiction, selfishness and unwillingness to become a responsible adult caused my second marriage to spiral downward. For the next several years, my wife and I were separated while I was lost in my addiction.

When my drug-sharing neighbor decided to move to San Antonio, Texas, I asked if I could tag along. It was one of many selfish choices I was to make in the years ahead. For the next six months, I covered a lot of ground in the "friendly" state, moving from town to town and from drug to drug. Finally, I caught wind of a sales job in Corpus Christi and decided to try my luck. I had no car and no money, so I headed for the highway to hitchhike my way to the coast.

It's probably clear to you by now that my life had zero direction in terms of plans or purpose. As I stood there on the road with my thumb out, a cattle truck pulled off to give me a ride. I climbed into the cab of the truck and quickly realized the driver didn't speak English. There was no seat on the passenger side of the cab, so while I bounced around silently on the metal floor, I had plenty of time to think about my circumstances. As we covered the miles, I had a "THAT moment," which forced me to be honest with myself, and it went something like this:

"Bill, what are you doing with your life? Why are you here? Because you are lazy! You don't want to work. You don't want to think. If you don't want to be in the same place this time next year, something has to change. You have to turn yourself around!"

I realized it was up to me and no one else.

That day I promised myself—not God, not my wife—that I would never be in that situation again. I wish I could say I came to my senses that day and gave up using drugs as part of my promise to myself. Instead, I became a functional addict, able to make a living, but still without direction or purpose in my life. Yet, I believe that even then, God was developing a skill in me that only he knew I'd need in order to reach my Promised Land.

The job in Corpus Christi was in sales. Buyer's clubs, which used the collective buying power of their members to purchase discounted and difficult-to-find products, were in their heyday in the 1970s. For the next few months, I moved between Corpus Christi, Dallas and Wharton, Texas, selling buyer's club memberships to ranchers and farmers. My life revolved around making money, staying high and driving miles of highway from one town or ranch to the next. I was still not on the right track. In fact, I was on no track at all.

Finally, just before Christmas in 1975, my personal roller coaster stopped just long enough for me to take another painful, but honest, look at myself. My employers had insisted that I come to Dallas for the company Christmas party that year—550 miles round-trip from Wharton, Texas, where I was living at the infamous landmark Tee Pee Motel.

On the return trip "home," my clunker of a car broke down. Penniless and stranded, I had plenty of time to take stock again:

"Bill, you are frustrated and exhausted. You are living out of a suitcase in a concrete tee pee. You are far away from your family, your friends, your wife and your daughter. You are in Wharton, Texas, for heaven's sake! What are you doing here?"

"THAT moment" sent me packing back to Louisville. I was still separated from my wife, so I humbled myself enough to ask my parents if I could move home.

Now, I can imagine what you are thinking:

This is the part where Bill Heintz remembers the way his parents brought him up.

And how God saved his life after the accident on the Autobahn. And how God healed his leg.

This is where Bill cries out to God and experiences some sort of life transformation.

No. This is where Bill Heintz, at 28 years old, moved into his mom and dad's house and continued living without direction or purpose. This is where using and abusing drugs continued to be the focus of my life. This is where I continued to ignore my second marriage. It is also where I failed to be a father to my sweet, beautiful little girl.

I had no job, a worthless car, and no life other than my efforts to find and use whatever drugs I could get my hands on. Disheartened and disappointed in me, my dad said the words no father wants to say and no son wants to hear:

"Bill, I'm afraid you're just never going to amount to much."

His words knocked me to the floor. Though I didn't stop popping pills right away, I'd still have to say I experienced a defining moment that day. I began taking stock of my life. I began to think beyond the drugs.

My dad's words brought me out of my stupor, and I determined I would get back on my feet and start working again. I picked up where I'd left off in Wharton, using my sales skills to build a career in a buyer's club in Louisville, Kentucky. Soon, I moved to Cincinnati and was offered my own franchise. I took this opportunity very seriously and began to work my way toward success. Within a few months, I was invited by a finance company to partner with them and start my own buyer's club. Within a year, we had stores in Canton, Cincinnati and Akron, Ohio.

By 1978, money flowed freely, but nothing else had really changed. Though I'd reconciled with my wife briefly (just long enough for her to become pregnant with our second daughter), I was nearing the end of our very broken marriage. I was still a functional drug addict and always high. I still lacked direction. No matter how many "THAT moments" had come my way, I still didn't recognize God's voice.

I couldn't hear him, because I simply wasn't listening.

"God's promised land offer does not depend on your perfection, it depends on his."

Max Lucado, "Glory Days"

A Path to Purpose

I've always imagined God shaking his head, and maybe rolling his eyes, at my inability to take a cue during those years. Thankfully, like the good father he is, he put someone squarely in my face who would help me recognize his voice and get me started on the long-neglected path and plan he had for my life.

Helena was an employee in my Canton store who showed her love for Jesus in everything she did. It occurred to me that she always seemed naturally high and in great spirits, while I had to buy drugs and put them in my body to get an artificial high. I have a personal belief that if I can find a better, easier way to do anything, I'll choose that way over something more difficult. So after months of observing Helena, my curiosity got the best of me, and I decided to start attending her church. It wasn't long before I responded to an altar call and accepted Jesus Christ as my Lord and Savior.

It was 1979, a pivotal year for me in many ways. My wife and I finally divorced after I had put her through eight painful years. I gave up drugs and gave in to Christ. I now knew and understood that God wanted me to fully surrender my life to his purpose and plan. And as I stood on the

threshold of the journey ahead, he brought a woman into my life who would become my partner, my challenger, my teacher and even my rescuer from time to time—my wife Michele.

I believe God knew I was too unequipped and disorganized for the plan he had for my life so he blessed me with this life partner and friend who would become the greatest inspiration and helpmate to me. On Christmas Eve day in 1980, Michele and I were married. It was one of the greatest "THAT moments" of my life.

Now the Lord had my full attention, and I was beginning to recognize his voice and direction. Though I was a very young Christian, I knew he was calling me into full-time ministry. I didn't know what kind of ministry it would be, but my heart and mind were open to whatever he wanted me to do and wherever he wanted me to go.

Once I realized I was really being called into the ministry, I had to learn to trust God. I had three strikes against me when it came to becoming a licensed pastor in my denomination: I was a former drug addict, I had no seminary education and I was divorced—twice.

But God was already speaking into my future. As I dived into his Word and learned to trust him with my life, I knew he could change others like he was changing me. I wanted to help lead others to the hope and purpose they would find in a personal relationship with Jesus Christ, but

I couldn't do it if I held on to the shame and regrets of my past. I realized the best way to take hold of the future God had in store for me was to let go of the past.

I had a job to do. I had a passion and a purpose for my life. I had to be somebody for him. I had to begin my journey toward my Promised Land. It was time to leave "you'll never amount to much" far behind and begin to walk in the opportunities God was opening up to me every single day.

Ours is not your typical love story.

Though we were both healing from broken relationships, and probably nowhere near ready to enter another, Bill and I took a chance and dated. Eight weeks later we were married. Our first year of marriage had its share of challenges, but it was also a beautifully significant year because I gave my life to the Lord shortly after our wedding day. God's grace permeated our marriage. As we learned how to live life as husband and wife, we had no idea he was also preparing us to be partners in ministry. How could God use two people with such brokenness, and so many failures and mistakes? It is simple yet profound: grace.

You see, not only does he forgive our debts—he makes all things new.

Michele

A Wave Goodbye

You have to leave the past behind before you can do what God wants you to do without the distraction of self-doubt. Paul says in Philippians 3:13-14 (NIV):

> **Brothers and sisters, I do not consider myself yet to have taken hold of it. But one thing I do: Forgetting what is behind and straining toward what is ahead, I press on toward the goal to win the prize for which God has called me heavenward in Christ Jesus.**

Now I'm going to give you a ridiculous, but very real example of what it is to "forget what is behind and strain toward what is ahead." By 1987, I'd made up my mind to minister to the down and out—folks who'd believed the lie that "they'd never amount to much."

God had been developing this vision for ministry in me through a series of experiences since I had accepted Christ back in 1979. I knew I wanted to help those who were addicted to drugs and alcohol. Now, he was about to shape that dream into what many years later would become The Foundry Ministries.

In the summer of 1987, Michele and I visited her family in Pompano Beach, Florida. One Sunday morning, Michele's sister-in-law told us about a recovery program called Faith Farm in Fort Lauderdale, where program participants worked in the ministry's various enterprises and shared responsibility for its upkeep. Intrigued, I made an appointment to visit Faith Farm the very next day. After I got off the phone, we loaded the kids in the car and headed to the beach.

I held my 2-year-old in my arms while we hollered and splashed and played in the ocean. I had just jumped one wave when another one smacked me hard from behind and knocked out my dentures.

Panic hit me. Holding my son high above the next wave, I gestured frantically to Michele to "Come get this kid!" At the same time, I stomped around hoping by some miracle my teeth had gotten caught in the seaweed beneath the water.

Several moments of searching turned up nothing, of course, but I couldn't give up. I turned to my beautiful wife, 14 years my junior, and asked, "Michele, how much do you love me? Would you go ask the lifeguard if anyone has turned in my teeth?"

Horrified, she responded with, "It all depends. Do I have to tell him you're my husband?"

We left the beach without my teeth that day and I've always wondered what happened to my dentures. Are they still drifting along the ocean floor? Are they now a home for some sea creature? Did they wash up on a beach somewhere along the Florida coast and traumatize some poor kid?

When Monday morning rolled around, as I began dressing for my meeting at Faith Farm, my wife and I had the following exchange:

"Where are you going?"

"I'm going to Faith Farm."

"Have you looked in the mirror? You have no teeth!"

"I bet some of the folks I'll see there won't have teeth, either."

Was I self-conscious that day? You bet! I'd looked in the mirror. I looked very different without my teeth. But my passion, coupled with what I believed was God's purpose for my life, got me to that appointment. As I toured Faith Farm, I had no idea God was showing me his vision of what would someday become The Foundry Ministries.

That day, my passion met God's purpose for my life and showed me my destiny.

Today, I can write with a more mature perspective on the "wave goodbye" and Faith Farm than I could have in 1987. But I must say at the shocking moment I saw Bill without his teeth on the beach, I was not happy! I wish I could say my heart bled with compassion to see someone without a necessary part of their appearance, but unfortunately I was more worried about the million deaths I was dying! Here we were on a crowded public beach in the middle of summer, and my strapping, young, handsome husband had no teeth!

I could have embraced or even been more proud of the horrific results of that ocean event had it been the result of a fight with a giant fish to save our toddler son. But no! The reality was far less valiant. He lost his teeth because a wave simply slapped him on the back. How unromantic!

So you can imagine my disbelief the next morning when Bill dressed for his appointment at Faith Farm. However, when the shock wore off, an overwhelming sense of security flooded my soul as I realized that my husband, the tenacious leader of our family

and ministry, would let nothing stand in the way of God's calling. His focus was on one thing, the Promised Land, and nothing was going to derail him on his journey.

In retrospect, I now thank God for the 'wave' that showed me the beautiful, vulnerable strength of this man whose faith was, and still is, unwavering. (No pun intended.)

Michele

Leaving It All Behind

The visit to Faith Farm was incredibly eye-opening. Men and women who had suffered years of addiction were putting the pieces of their lives back together through Christ-centered programs that combined Bible study, counseling, life skills and hard work. I remembered the times in the cattle truck and on the road, when I'd berated myself about my laziness and the need to work and earn my own way.

Now I recognized those times as "THAT moments" in my life. My visit to Faith Farm confirmed that God had been speaking into my life even in my addiction and now was showing me a glimpse of his vision for my Promised Land.

Once I saw what God was doing at Faith Farm, (www.faithfarm.org) which is still going strong today with several campuses serving homeless and addicted men and women in Florida, I knew there was no turning back. I gladly put the mistakes I had made before I came to Christ behind me. I became determined and committed to the journey ahead. The Apostle Paul's commitment inspired and encouraged me when he said: "I press on toward the goal to win the prize for which God has called me heavenward in Christ Jesus." Philippians 3:14 (NIV)

Through my experience of visiting Faith Farm without my teeth—and through many more experiences since then that required humility—I've learned that my attitude is everything.

I've learned that if I think I can, I will. If I think I can't, I won't.

It's that simple.

It's likely that in your journey, as in mine, God's calling on your life is not part-time or short-term, but rather, it's for eternity. In your journey, you *will* face adversity in many forms, no doubt about it. The key to overcoming it is to commit and entrust your lifelong journey to the One who created you. Without that commitment and trust, it's easy to lose sight of the prize.

Though the years following our visit to Faith Farm would bring more adversity our way, Michele and I clung to Hebrews 10:35-36 (NIV), which says: Do not throw away your confidence; it will be richly rewarded. You need to persevere so that when you have done the will of God, you will receive what he has promised.

God keeps his promises. His promise for your life will become a reality if you trust, believe and obey him. It doesn't matter how you start out. Leave it behind! What does matter is how you finish. Be confident that he has plans for you, and his promises will come true.

"*Destiny is no matter of chance.*
It is a matter of choice:
It is not a thing to be waited for, it is a
   thing to be achieved."

William Jennings Bryan

Just Say "YES"

I hear voices. They come from the people around me—people I love, people I respect, people who need me, people I need. There are voices I listen to (my wife) and those that I ignore (men's moisturizer commercials). There are voices that jolt me and voices whose words leave me hurting and confused. But in the middle of it all, there is my own voice and there is the voice of God.

I can't think of a single person who is not surrounded by a company of voices: some negative, some positive, some helpful, some you wish would simply go away! No matter who you are, what your Promised Land looks like and what your plan is to get there, you have to know how to separate God's voice from the others, including your own.

After I gave my heart to Christ, it was imperative that I learned to hear God's voice above all the other noise, especially above my own thoughts. I knew I wanted to minister to people. God knew who those people were and what my ministry would be.

In 1987, just months before what is now known as The Denture Incident, I was sitting in a gutter in downtown Louisville having a "THAT

moment" next to a guy named Jason. Now, how we got to Louisville from Cincinnati doesn't make a whole lot of sense. As a matter of fact, a lot of the routes I took to get to my Promised Land don't make sense. That's why hearing God's voice and knowing that it's really his is incredibly important.

Back in 1984, God directed me to resign from my job in Cincinnati, but he didn't tell me what to do or where to go after I did. When my boss asked why I was resigning, the only answer I could give him was, "God told me to." Though that answer didn't satisfy my boss, Michele was solidly on board because she knew God had spoken clearly to me.

For two months after I resigned, we lived on our savings, confident that God would show us what our next step needed to be and where he wanted us to go. We'd lived in Cincinnati for three years and life had been very good for us. The job I had just left paid well, and Michele had been able to be what she loved most, a stay-at-home mom. We loved our church and enjoyed fellowship with the many friends we'd made. In fact, Michele and I had been hosting a Bible study in our home. My first preaching experience took place in one of those Bible studies, expounding from my "pulpit"—the back of a brown tweed chair. Michele was from Ohio and her family was there. It was also where I first got the desire to minister through preaching God's Word. We loved our life there.

But God had something greater for us, and we knew it was even more important than the comfortable lifestyle and friends we'd acquired in Cincinnati. Wherever he took us next, we trusted him fully and were ready and willing to go.

Nothing materialized! As the time passed and our savings dwindled, I began to look for another job in Cincinnati, but had a surprisingly difficult time finding opportunities. During the only interview I could get, I was offered a position selling vending machines … in Louisville. Hmm. Just a few months earlier at Christmastime, Michele and I had visited my family in Louisville, and we dreamed together about living closer to my daughters, parents and siblings.

Well, okay, we would move to Louisville, and I would sell vending machines. We had no idea why God wanted us to make the move, but it didn't matter. As we'd grown in our faith, our priorities had changed from secular to spiritual. Money was no longer a motivator for me; the call to minister had taken its place.

After reading what I've just written, I can understand why many people would question my actions. Why did I think God was motivating us to move to Louisville? How could Michele say "YES" to moving farther away from her family? What could I point to that would prove he was in our decision at all?

All I can say is that Michele and I believed he was directing us toward the move to Louisville. The experiences we had there, and in the years afterward, confirmed we were indeed hearing his voice.

We were in good company. I could compare our experience with Abram's own in Genesis 12:1-4 (NIV):

> **The Lord had said to Abram, "Go from your country, your people and your father's household to the land I will show you. I will make you into a great nation, and I will bless you; I will make your name great, and you will be a blessing. I will bless those who bless you, and whoever curses you I will curse; and all peoples on earth will be blessed through you." So Abram went, as the Lord had told him and Lot went with him.**

God told Abram to pack his bags and go. "Abram went, as the Lord had told him," and so did we. Throughout all the years Michele and I have been together, we've agreed that when God says move, we move—whether that means relocating, doing something new or simply getting out of the way.

Once we'd settled into our home in Louisville, we joined a nearby church and wondered what God had in store for us. I was impatient to get into ministry and it wasn't long before God brought me an exciting opportunity.

Early in 1987, our pastors' wives attended a leadership conference led by Pastor Tommy Barnett, co-founder of The Dream Center Network of ministries (www.dreamcenter.org), which today has more than 100 outreaches nationwide and internationally. The ladies came back from the conference, and they were excited at the prospect of sharing Christ, as well as practical assistance and spiritual help with the down-and-out people of our city. Their excitement was contagious, spreading throughout our church leadership, and my pastor asked me to join the staff part-time to coordinate a street ministry of our own. Given my past struggle with drugs and the life that went with them, he felt I would be perfect to head up this new outreach.

I was delighted that he was willing to take a chance on me, but to be honest, I just wasn't interested in helping people with addictions. I'd put that life behind me, and I didn't want to re-enter the drug world with all the apathy and failure that went with it. My solution was to accept the job, but lead from a distance. In retrospect, I thought I could minister without ministering.

My plan for our first night out was this: I would go downtown with the two guys who'd signed up for the new outreach, one an ex-alcoholic and one an ex-convict, and get them started. Then, I'd head home.

Our first stop (and the only one I planned to make) was the Louisville Rescue Mission (www.louisvillerescuemission.org), which is the fifth-oldest rescue mission in the United States and provides emergency relief services, recovery programs and more to homeless men and women. We went inside and talked to some homeless guys about attending our church, then left the building and walked to Market Street a block away. Just as I was about to make my getaway, I noticed two guys sitting in the gutter drinking. A minute later, I found myself sitting in the gutter, too.

For the next four hours, I talked to Jason while his drinking buddy dozed beside us. My inhibitions and fears fell away as we conversed, and I realized we were kindred spirits. I understood what he was going through. I could connect with him. Most of all, I realized that I was contented and fulfilled as I sat in that gutter—in fact, I was happier than I'd been in a long time.

In those hours, God broke me and spoke to me. His voice was urgent, "Will you help me bring these people out of bondage?" Driving home, sometime around midnight, I answered his call and said, "YES, Lord."

*"Most big cities have a skid row—
an area beset with flophouses,
crack houses, rundown bars, and
abandoned buildings. It's where
the observable homeless tend to
congregate, often sitting or laying
on the sidewalks, or traversing the
concrete like zombies on patrol. It's
a place where raw emotions rest
precariously close to the surface."*

John Ashmen, "Invisible Neighbors"

The Trouble with YES

Saying "YES" to God opens a person up to a lot of adventure, a lot of contentment, and a whole lot of trouble. After I said "YES" to building a ministry that would help free people who were enslaved to addiction, my life did not take a suddenly straight path to The Foundry Ministries. Far from it! Frankly, I wasn't sure I was up to what I believed God had in store for me, and I sure didn't know there was a decade-long journey ahead before I would set foot in my Promised Land.

The Old Testament is filled with stories of people God used to do incredible things even though they felt, and were, totally unequipped for the task and had no idea what kind of journey they'd signed up for. So while I felt I had little to offer the Lord, I knew many of my Bible heroes had felt the same way.

In Exodus 3 and 4, God asked Moses to join him and free the Israelites who were enslaved in Egypt. Moses came up with all kinds of excuses as to why God had chosen the wrong guy. He was scared. He felt completely unqualified. My version of their conversation goes something like this:

God: "Moses, I have found the man who will free my people from their bondage in Egypt."

Moses: "That's great, God! Who is it?"

God: "It's you, Moses."

Moses: "But God, I am an old man. I am a fugitive and a murderer. I can't lead anybody! How am I supposed to pull this off?"

God: "What's in your hand?"

Moses: "It's a stick … a staff."

God: "It's mine now. Watch this! (ZAP—the staff is now a snake!) Moses, pick that snake up by the tail."

Moses (grabs the snake and it turns back to a staff): "But God, I can't speak very well. Please send someone else."

God (now angry): "That's no excuse. Go anyway! I'll send Aaron to speak for you. Now go!"

The Bible says: "So Moses took his wife and sons, put them on a donkey and started back to Egypt. And he took the staff of God in his hand." Exodus 4:20 (NIV)

This verse may seem insignificant, but it says something powerful about what happens to us when we, inadequacies and all, take what little we have and give it to God. When Moses finally decides to say "YES, Lord," and accepts the vision God has for his life, the stick becomes "the staff of God."

That staff now represented the power and authority of God!

David, a teenaged shepherd boy, fought a heavily armored, giant warrior named Goliath with only a slingshot and stone, in I Samuel 17. Goliath probably looked down and said to himself: "This is absurd. This guy is just a little runt! My armor probably weighs more than he does!"

But God knew David was no runt. He saw him very differently.

To God, David was a king.

David might have been thinking this way as he faced the giant: "Big man, you are coming to me with all this experience. You are big and tall. You are well equipped and have more experience than I do. But I have God. I've already seen God kill the bear and the lion. You are just the next big thing in line."

David defeated Goliath. It was a great feat followed by more and greater feats. So great, in fact, that King Saul became jealous of the humble hero and tried repeatedly to kill David. Though Saul chased David

over hills, through caves and into various countries, David was loyal and honorable to the end, and became king of Israel after Saul's death.

As a teenager, David heard God say, "I have the plan, and you have to be the man." That day, David said, "YES, Lord" and never looked back, despite his size and the seemingly inadequate tools at his disposal.

With these examples and so many others under my belt, I was fairly confident that God would equip me for the long haul (though I'm glad, in retrospect, that I had no idea how long that haul would be).

Our ministry to the homeless and addicted people on the streets of Louisville took off after the night I spoke with Jason. Each week, we headed out to invite people to our Sunday church services with the promise that we would feed them breakfast and provide them with lunch before returning them downtown. Soon, we were bussing up to 50 people to our church on Sundays. As we got to know each person better and heard their stories, we found it heartbreaking to return them to the streets, so we began providing shelter for some of them in a house on the church property.

Jason, my friend from the gutter, decided to come to church one Sunday. The day he asked Christ to become his Savior was one of unsurpassed joy! Just a month later, the impact of God's calling on my life really hit home when Jason died of sclerosis of the liver.

Jason's death was a "THAT moment" as I realized that, if I had not said "YES" to the Lord, if I had not had that encounter with Jason in the gutter, Jason might not have been ushered into heaven a few weeks later.

That pivotal moment showed me that, though I did not think I had much to offer, God could use whatever I had to help others find Jesus. I simply had to give him all that I had and he would take care of the rest.

As the weeks flew by, more and more people in the church got involved in the street ministry. Many had never reached out to the hurting in this way and their enthusiasm was contagious. It was during this time that Michele and I visited Faith Farm. When we returned home to Louisville, we dreamed of expanding the ministry to include some kind of enterprise where we could employ the homeless, teaching them the value of work and a job well done. They would be the stockholders, using their skills and talents to benefit themselves and others.

Frankly, during those months, I believed that, in many ways, I had reached my Promised Land. Though I was still working full-time in sales to support our family, I was content and satisfied in a way I had never known before. We were seeing amazing results among the homeless people we were working with. But as it turned out, the church's street ministry was only a training ground, a stopping point on a much longer journey.

"You may not control all the events that happen to you, but you can decide not to be reduced by them."

Maya Angelou, "Letter to My Daughter"

Shattered

Six months into our work with the street ministry, my pastor's wife asked me how it was going, and I responded enthusiastically, "Wonderful! I believe the church's 10-acre property isn't big enough for what God is going to do here someday."

That afternoon, my pastor called me into his office and said eight words that made no sense to me at all: "I think it's time for us to part." I was so shocked I could not think of a response.

Before I left the campus, he allowed me to go talk to the men I had grown so close to through the street ministry and let them know I would no longer be working with them. Their responses ranged from disbelief to deep sadness to anger.

Confused and devastated, I headed home to tell Michele and the children we would not be returning to the church. Afterward, as I sat on our porch thinking back over the past six months, I felt penalized for doing the best I could have done.

As people in our church wondered about my absence, some called and some stopped by our house to ask what had happened. Staff members

were told not to contact us, which made us feel ostracized, exiled—as though something immoral had happened. My reply to those who got in touch with us was that I did not agree with the decision and that they should talk to the pastor if they had any questions.

This experience presented one very long, defining moment for me.

Though my heart was deeply injured, I was determined not to cause strife within the church body because we loved not only our church, but our pastor and his wife, too. Still, the weight of what had happened was crushing, and I could not seem to get out from under it.

Michele encouraged me to go to a nearby prayer retreat aptly called Prayer Mountain. For three days, I wrestled with the Lord there. At one point, I cried out to God, "Why did you let this happen?" He responded with "Trust me." Later, I cried out again, "You could have prevented this." This time he said, "Trust me; don't lean on your own understanding." I tried to trust, but I was just too broken. I could not get from where I was to where God wanted me to be.

Returning home, I learned more devastating news. All of the men the church had been housing had taken off and returned to the streets. One of them, Curtis, had become a very dear friend to Michele and me. Days after I was let go, Curtis was drinking heavily again. One night, when he could not get to an open liquor store, he drank after-

shave in a last-ditch effort to get alcohol into his system. A day later he died.

Michele and I were rocked to the core by these tragic experiences. So much so that I almost gave up the journey. We packed up the kids soon after I was fired and moved to Knoxville. Then we moved on to Oak Ridge and finally to Decatur. For three years, we changed course again and again, finding healing in different ministries, and trying to find that elusive contentment we had known before.

The pain of our experience in the Louisville church was unbearable and affected our whole family. How do you explain to your young children that you can't go back to the church you love? Our church wasn't just a building—the people there were our family. Depression, sadness, despair, confusion and resentment held my soul captive. The pastor's wife was my best friend and my first mentor. I adored her and looked up to her. Now we felt exiled from the people we loved so dearly.

Our family moved to Knoxville, Tennessee, three months after Bill was fired. I was depressed beyond words. We were living in a new city and state while my whole life and heart was still in Louisville, Kentucky. I could relate to David, the psalmist, and read the Psalms day after day. One day, I cried out to the Lord and asked that he would impress on my friend's (the pastor's wife) heart to call me. And she called that day! In that sweet moment I experienced the loving kindness, tenderness and compassion of the Lord as he answered the very specific cry of my broken heart. To me, it was the promise of healing.

Michele

I can't begin to express the pain I heard time and time again in Bill and Michele's voices as they shared their experience at the church in Louisville, Kentucky. As a Midwesterner, I was writing this book from long distance and most of our interviews occurred over our cell phones—Bill in his porch swing and I on my own front porch in Kansas City. At one point, when I sent the text on that experience to Bill for review, he said, "I am really struggling with the fact that I can't get across to you just how painful, how shattering this was for us. I wish you could see my face as I tell you about it."

I began to realize that Bill and Michele wanted readers to have a clear understanding of just how painful a "YES" journey can be, that saying "YES" to God's vision for your life can bring a lot of trouble along the way and must come with conviction that, no matter what, you—with your Father beside you—will see the journey through.

Bill repeatedly brought up the song "He'll Do it Again," written by Dawn Thomas and performed by one of his favorite singers, Karen Wheaton, as one that gave his family comfort and strength through these and other hard times. Here is a YouTube link to Karen singing it.

http://bit.ly/Wheaton-DoItAgain

Author's Note from Julie

"When you first respond to God …

you are bringing about the birth of your vision.

And like everything else in the kingdom of God,

a birth is followed by a death, and then by a resurrection.

Every one of God's visions and dreams goes through this

process of birth, death, and resurrection."

Jentezen Franklin, "Believe That You Can"

This quote means a lot to me because I experienced it first-hand. In Louisville, I experienced the birth and death of my vision. It was resurrected in Bessemer almost a decade later when I became executive director of what is today The Foundry Ministries.

Bill

YES with Conviction

During those years of suffering and wondering, I learned something about the perseverance of God. And I learned the importance of saying "YES" with conviction.

Like I said, after I was fired, I really wanted to throw in the towel. But God did not feel the same way at all! While I was discouraged and confused, he was still counting on my "YES." He wasn't discouraged or confused, and he wasn't giving up. I'm pretty sure giving up is not even in God's vocabulary. And he was not going to let it be part of mine.

God looks for people who will say "YES" with conviction. When I said "YES" after sitting in the gutter with Jason, I believed I meant it with all my heart. I could not foresee the dangers and barriers in the road ahead, but God could. He knew what I was up against, and he was ready for it.

Here is the thing about conviction: it does not let you go. In fact, I believe conviction is the glue that holds a person's journey together when things just do not make sense.

I cannot stress enough that if you are on an intentional journey—a journey that comes from saying "YES, Lord" to a vision he has cast for

your life, you will encounter naysayers, wrong turns, potholes and barriers. Did I say potholes? I should have said chasms. Did I say barriers? Perhaps mountains would be more like it!

But when God calls us to a journey and the going gets really hard, it is conviction that keeps us on the road. It is conviction that pulls you through a "THAT moment" which could move you forward or cause you to leave the road behind.

Conviction is the voice that does not go away no matter what. It is not hindered by economic hardship or puzzling circumstances or even heartbreak. It does not say, "Oh, I wasn't expecting that. That really hurt! Never mind."

As Michele and I moved from city to city, we continued to hold to the conviction that we were to be in full-time ministry. Even when I felt defeated, the idea just would not let me go.

I had said "YES" in that gutter in Louisville and the vision had been cast at Faith Farm. When I thought about quitting or going off in another direction, I had no peace. When our emotions tried to dictate our next steps, the Word told Michele and me to:

Trust God from the bottom of your heart; don't try to figure out everything on your own. Listen for God's voice in everything you do,

everywhere you go; he's the one who will keep you on track. Proverbs 3:5-6 (The Message)

As we turned to the Bible for support, God reminded us of the three young Hebrew noblemen, Shadrach, Meshach and Abednego, who were living in Babylon under the reign of King Nebuchadnezzar. When the king commanded everyone to bow before a huge golden idol he had created, the three men were loyal to the God of Israel and calmly refused to bow. Nebuchadnezzar was outraged and commanded that the three be thrown into a fiery furnace unless they backed down, taunting them with, "What god will be able to save you from my hands?"

The Hebrews replied in Daniel 3:16-18 (NIV):

> **King Nebuchadnezzar, we do not need to defend ourselves before you in this matter. If we are thrown into the blazing furnace, the God we serve is able to deliver us from it, and he will deliver us from Your Majesty's hand. But even if he does not, we want you to know, Your Majesty, that we will not serve your gods or worship the image of gold you have set up.**

That is the kind of conviction I believe God wants from each one of us. It is a belief that will not let you go. It lines up with God's word and it lines up with what you feel you must do no matter what the

situation looks like on the surface. This kind of conviction will not let you turn in another direction, regardless of what you may encounter on the road ahead.

A simple formula stands out to me as I write this, which will help you through "THAT moment" and the resulting decision you make:

When your "YES" is followed by the kind of conviction that will not let you go, that "YES" is the road to your Promised Land.

If you are able to give up and walk away at peace with yourself and God at some point, it is likely your destination was not one of God's calling.

When Michele and I followed our conviction, when we remained true to the "YES," we were at peace. In Philippians 4:5-7 (NIV), Paul assures the Philippian church that:

> **The Lord is near. Do not be anxious about anything, but in every situation, by prayer and petition, with thanksgiving, present your requests to God. And the peace of God, which transcends all understanding, will guard your hearts and your minds in Christ Jesus.**

We had plenty of reasons for anxiety during those three years we spent moving from place to place in Tennessee, but thankfully, we had plenty

of reasons for praise, too. With each healing step, we found our way back to the road toward the Promised Land.

"When we realize and embrace the Lord's will for us, we will love to do it. We won't want to do anything else. It's a passion."

Franklin Graham

Forgiveness

Getting back on the road again could have gone two ways for the Heintz family: We could have seen the way ahead through a haze of bitterness and anger, or we could continue our journey with avid anticipation and with our eyes on a Father we knew to be loving and trustworthy. At first, the choice was clouded with confusion and grief, but as we contemplated picking up the journey again, we knew we needed to see the future with clear eyes and clear consciences just as Paul instructs in Acts 24:16 (NIV) when he says, "I strive always to keep my conscience clear before God and man."

Here is what we were discovering: You cannot explore the road ahead, you cannot be excited about tomorrow if you have not forgiven for what happened to you yesterday. In fact, you cannot move forward at all, because lack of forgiveness is a roadblock—a brick wall—and until you tear it down, you are just stuck.

A few weeks after I was fired, I realized I had a problem. I found myself constantly obsessing and agonizing over what had happened in my pastor's office. I went over and over the one-sided conversation that had taken place. The conversation had come out of nowhere. In fact, I had

been so shocked I had not even tried to defend myself or change his mind.

I tried to pray and to read my Bible, but to no avail. I could not concentrate on anything. Something had to happen or I would never be able to move forward into whatever future God had in mind for us. Finally, I decided that Michele and I would have to have one more conversation with the pastor and his wife if I was ever going to put this disappointment behind me.

Our hope was that we could resolve the conflict with this couple who had meant so much to us. They had given me my first opportunity to experience transformative ministry to the homeless and addicted, and Michele and I loved them dearly. As we made our way to the appointment, I envisioned a time of honest conversation ending in a few tears, maybe a hug and, hopefully, reconciliation.

Well, the meeting did not go as we had hoped at all. During our short, uncomfortable talk, nothing was resolved. As we said our goodbyes, I knew I could not walk out the way I had walked in. I also knew it would do no good to tell them "I forgive you" because they felt there was nothing to forgive.

Just outside the office door, I resolved in my heart that I would forgive them right then and there. I realized that if I did not forgive them I would owe a debt to the Lord who had forgiven me of so many, many sins, and I was determined to walk out of that church debt-free.

Looking back, I am so grateful that the Lord laid it on my heart to forgive.

I believe God was asking me at that moment, "Bill, can I trust you with the vision I have for you?" I realized he could not entrust his vision to someone who could not forgive because there would be many times ahead when I would need to forgive (and be forgiven).

I was not the only person set free when I forgave the pastor and his wife. I've learned that forgiveness is made up of three elements.

- An injury

- A debt resulting from the injury

- The cancellation of the debt

When one person injures another person in any way, he or she owes the injured person a debt. Unfortunately, not everyone who does harm recognizes the injury, and the hurt goes unresolved because no one apologizes; no one asks forgiveness. Unresolved injuries can conjure up all kinds of negativity, the kind you carry with you unless you take the steps needed to resolve the debt once and for all.

A debt like that can only be forgiven when you free your debtor of his or her obligation to pay you back, or even to admit a wrong. The debtor

may never know the debt has been canceled, but you do! Canceling the debt does even more; it frees you to stop dwelling on what is owed to you. That day, as Michele and I walked back to our car, we were able to simply love our friends and move on with hearts free of bitterness and resentment. The debt was canceled, and we could go forward into whatever the Lord had for us without holding on to the hurt we had experienced.

I've learned that when we fail to forgive, we cannot accept the blessings of tomorrow because we continue to live in the curses, disappointment and pain of yesterday. When we fail to forgive, we live in resentment, which breeds anger, which breeds bitterness.

Bitterness is a horrendous tool the devil loves to use against us. Bitterness is destructive, debilitating and demoralizing. In Hebrews 12:14-15 (NIV), Paul encourages the Hebrews to:

> **Make every effort to live in peace with everyone and to be holy; without holiness no one will see the Lord. See to it that no one falls short of the grace of God and that no bitter root grows up to cause trouble and defile many.**

If you have been hurt deeply by someone, then you know that bitterness sours and spoils your anticipation of anything good. It hinders you from having peace and becoming everything God created you to be.

The lenses of bitterness keep you in the dark, blinding you to all the good things the Lord has in store for you to experience and accomplish. Bitterness is a force that takes away your ability to hope. It keeps you stuck in a pain-filled yesterday so you can't envision what God has for you tomorrow.

Do not let the pain of yesterday define who you become tomorrow.

Bitterness is a root, and it is very much alive. The more you feed it with anger and jealousy and unforgiveness, the more it grows. It refuses to allow you to believe in what is possible. In fact, it holds you in a place of negativity and will not let you walk free toward your Promised Land. And that is why it has to die.

Making the decision to forgive allows healing to begin so you can move forward. In my own experience, deciding to forgive was a sign to the Lord and to myself that I could handle what he had envisioned for my life.

I don't think I am overstating it to say that if I had not worked through the pain and anger of being fired; if I had let unforgiveness and bitterness take root in my soul; and if I had refused to cancel a debt my friends did not know they owed, my journey to my Promised Land may have taken a serious detour. Like the Israelites, I may have wasted years journeying through a wilderness of my own making and never set foot into my Promised Land at all.

If you have been harmed by someone else's neglect, mistake, unkindness or misuse of power, understand that you have a choice. You do not have to forgive. You may not want to forgive. But if you choose to forgive, sincerely, you are set free to hope and dream again.

Sometimes it is hard to forgive because we are afraid it will send the wrong message; that we have condoned someone's wrongdoing or given them power of some kind. Do not let this way of thinking keep you in bondage. Forgiveness is not agreeing that what they did was right. It is agreeing to set yourself free.

Your responsibility is to forgive; the way the other person responds to that forgiveness is up to him or her.

One more thing: If you are to be a leader or hold a position of responsibility, whether at home, at work, or in your church, you must be able to forgive and to ask for forgiveness, because you are going to make mistakes. As the executive director of The Foundry Ministries, in my own Promised Land, I have experienced many moments of hurt. I have had to have the ability to confront a variety of painful situations and forgive time and again.

You are going to take some hits on your journey, and you have to find a way to resolve each situation and go forward. If you do not learn to roll with the punches, and you harbor unforgiveness, you cannot move forward on your journey or be a positive leader.

I cannot count the times I have had to go to a staff member or program participant and apologize for something I did or failed to do. Each time, two things happened because I was willing to admit I had made a mistake: First, I freed myself from being a hypocrite, someone willing to forgive, but unwilling to admit my own errors. And second, the person I wronged was able to trust and respect me because he or she saw I was willing to be truthful and humble myself.

One of the little things I have to offer the staff at The Foundry Ministries is to be a positive leader. Being a positive leader requires a person to have a positive attitude, and that is really important if you want to keep the good people you've hired! Frankly, I believe my staff would not stick around if they sensed a lack of forgiveness or humility in me, because they understand it would hinder the work God has given us to do.

Actually, "hinder" isn't a strong enough word. In the ministry of leadership, unforgiveness destroys! Consider how many people have left their churches because a lack of forgiveness has splintered the body. People in leadership are often admired and loved and trusted. The failure of a leader to ask forgiveness or to forgive is a destructive force that affects everyone around them. If you as a leader have allowed resentment, anger and bitterness to take root in your ministry, kill it now through the act of forgiveness.

Cancel the debt and set your ministry free!

About a year after that difficult conversation with our pastor and his wife, the four of us got together, and the first thing my former pastor shared was the regret of his decision to fire me. Because I had forgiven him, I could say with sincerity, "We all make mistakes." Though we seldom see each other, our continued friendship has been a wonderful result of forgiveness and reconciliation.

Bill

"In Louisville, when everything went haywire and I asked God why, he said, "Trust me."

Though nothing made sense, I had to trust him because I wasn't trustworthy to make right decisions at the time.

There are times when, if we aren't careful, we allow our emotions to dictate our actions.

Sometimes the situations we find ourselves in scream at us!

That screaming is the voice of fear. Watch out!

Fear has a way of putting on the brakes.

That's when we have to recognize God's voice and his power to take what is happening—as bad as it may be—and make it into something good as only he can do. Paul explains this in Romans 8:28 (NIV) which says:

'And we know that in all things God works for the good of those who love him, who have been called according to his purpose.'"

Bill

Detour to Decatur

I have to admit, I was simply uncertain about what and where God wanted me to be. I was certain of my calling but unsure of the direction and how it would apply to my life.

In the years after our departure from Louisville, Michele and I had often prayed a simple prayer: "God, we are on standby. Let your will be done. Open the door to whatever you have for us, and we will pack our bags and go."

Even though I had said "YES" to working with the homeless and addicted, and could still remember the contentment and satisfaction I had known during that six months in Louisville, I could not allow myself to dwell on it. I had not lost the vision, but I had to leave room for the possibility that God had another ministry in mind.

After three years of volunteering in various part-time ministries, my "YES" to full-time ministry was alive and well. In fact, I was itching to get to it. I continued to work in sales to support our growing family, but I also kept waiting and wondering what our next step was supposed to be. I knew God had mapped out a destination and there were still miles

of travel ahead of us. Everything in me cried out to get back on the road toward my vision. But how?

In April 1990, God answered that question through Chris, a youth pastor and friend from our church back in Louisville. Michele and I were just settling our family into a house in Oak Ridge, Tennessee, and I was volunteering in a church ministry to the elderly in the community. It was good work and important, but I knew it was only temporary—another pit stop on the road.

One evening, Chris called to let me know he had left his position as youth pastor at the Louisville church and was now working at Calvary Assembly (http://www.calvaryassembly.org) in Decatur, Alabama, under the leadership of its founder and senior pastor, George Sawyer. Chris described Calvary Assembly as a growing and outreach-oriented church. Church members went into government-housing communities, reaching out to bring relief to the hurting and vulnerable families living on the edge of poverty. I could hear the enthusiasm in Chris's voice, and my ears, and my hopes, perked up. Something powerful was going on at Calvary Assembly—something that took me back to the vision in Louisville and Faith Farm!

During our conversation, I admitted my own frustration at not being in full-time ministry. Though Chris knew there were no positions open at

the church, he still encouraged me to get in touch with Pastor Sawyer just to talk. What could I lose?

Days later, I headed for Decatur and my appointment with Calvary's pastor. As we discussed the direction of the church and the potential for its growing outreaches to the community, I realized George Sawyer was a man I could respect and work under.

"What is God calling you to do, Bill?" he asked. I knew where my heart was, but I was no longer certain God wanted me to work with the homeless and addicted, so I kept my response simple and open: "Pastor, I want to be in the ministry. Whatever you need me to do, I'll do it."

As we neared the end of my appointment, Pastor Sawyer told me he would like to have us move to Decatur, but there were no guarantees of employment at the church. "If it's God's will that we put you on staff, we will," he said, "but we are in a building project right now so it would be tough."

That was enough for me. When I got home that afternoon, I told Michele we needed to move to Decatur. Believe it or not, Michele was willing to pick up, pack up and move again! I took a job in Decatur selling real estate franchises and waited for an opportunity at the church to open up.

Three months later, Pastor Sawyer called to ask us to lead a Bible study for divorced and single men and women attending Calvary. We started our first Bible study in our home with around 12 people eager for guidance and fellowship. Six weeks later, we outgrew our living room and moved the study to a nearby restaurant. The months flew by as Michele and I grew to love our new friends and the ministry opportunities God brought our way.

As Christmas approached that year, we looked for new opportunities to serve in our church. Calvary had an outreach to prison inmates in a work release program in Decatur, and several came to church services on Sunday and Wednesday nights. Michele and I had invited four of the guys to our home for Thanksgiving dinner. It had been a great experience for our new friends, and it was sweetly reminiscent of our Louisville days with Curtis and Jason. Now it occurred to me that we could do even more!

When I asked our pastor if we could have a "Dinner for Jesus and His Friends" at Christmastime, he enthusiastically agreed. Our Thanksgiving dinner for four quickly gave way to Christmas dinner for hundreds as I asked Pastor Sawyer if we could include one group after another.

All the folks from the work release program?

Of course.

Families and the elderly living in government housing?

Sure.

How about the people from the nearby rescue missions and shelters?

Absolutely!

We scheduled our party for Saturday, December 22, and our plans included a huge holiday meal and exciting entertainment, along with loads of gifts, games and a puppet show for kids. The event grew, and I got my first taste of fundraising on a large scale. But, as a career salesman, asking for volunteer help, food and all the other things we would need was right up my alley.

Our church was primed for an outreach like this. People volunteered to bring holiday food like turkey, mashed potatoes and other traditional dishes. Restaurants also got into the act, donating corn on the cob and desserts. We held planning meetings for the dozens of volunteers who had signed up to help. We rented busses to bring in folks from the housing projects. We had even snagged Karen Wheaton, an amazing gospel singer and founder of The Ramp (www.theramp.org), a church in Hamilton, Alabama, to provide entertainment.

The day would be packed with activities. Impoverished families were invited to a midday feast followed by activities for kids and a puppet

show. During the evening, we would welcome men from the local rescue mission and work release program for a big dinner and concert with Karen Wheaton.

By the night before our "Dinner for Jesus and His Friends," we had invited hundreds of guests, checked our food lists, surveyed the banquet hall, confirmed our volunteers and everything was set and ready to go.

And then the rain began.

Just after midnight, and all through the day of the event, torrents of rain fell, washing out roads and bridges, flooding basements and cutting off electricity to hundreds of homes. By the time it stopped, we learned that 10 inches of rain had fallen in a single day—a record for that part of the state.

As you can imagine, waking up to a record-breaking rainfall and all its implications made for a bleak and disappointing morning. One by one, volunteers called to cancel, saying they had no way to get to the church. Folks who had committed to bringing roast turkey and other essentials were stranded, unable to cross bridges washed out by the flooding. Officials at the work release program called to say that, under the circumstances, transporting inmates to our Christmas dinner was not a good idea; they would be staying home for dinner.

No! What a disappointment. We'd planned everything right down to the last detail, but we had not been able to plan perfect weather. "Christmas Dinner for Jesus and His Friends" was not happening—his friends were not going to show up.

Then suddenly, everything changed! Many of our volunteers and cooks managed to find their way to the church despite the storm and muddy messes it was causing. The bus company came through, unloading 300 moms, dads and children from nearby government housing projects for lunch. The afternoon spilled over with laughter and joy as families shared in the food, puppet show and Christmas gifts! What had started as a dreary day ended with smiles all around as they boarded the busses for home.

Then at 4 p.m., an official from the work release program called to say their kitchen was flooded. Could their people come after all? We had barely hung up the phone before more busses pulled in, loaded with solemn-faced homeless men from the rescue mission in downtown Huntsville.

By the end of the day, more than 700 hungry men, women and children had made their way to Calvary Assembly's "Dinner for Jesus and His Friends." For hours, the hall was electric with color and laughter, music and energy. Moms, dads, children, inmates, the elderly, the homeless, our

volunteers—people whose lives would rarely coincide—celebrated the birth of Christ together.

As the party ended, our "friends of Jesus" who had arrived with such solemn faces boarded the busses for the return trip to the rescue mission singing Christmas carols. Our volunteers headed home exhausted but incredibly blessed by their experiences. Tearfully and gratefully, Michele and I again experienced the joy of bringing hope and the love of Christ to the hurting and the lonely. It was the best Christmas gift we could have received.

Sunday morning, the rain was forgotten and the excitement in our church was off the charts. The church had come alive in a whole new way! Everyone who had been involved in the dinner wanted to share his or her experiences. Finally someone said what everyone was feeling: "We never want to go through another Christmas without having 'Dinner for Jesus and His Friends.'" (True to that sentiment, Calvary Assembly continues to reach out to homeless and impoverished men, women and children through Christmas programs inspired by that first "Dinner with Jesus and His Friends.")

A couple weeks after the event, Pastor Sawyer called me into his office to talk. It was one of those amazing "THAT moments"—the conversation I'd been awaiting for years!

"Bill, you know we're in the middle of a building campaign, and we can't afford to bring you on staff," he said. "But with what you bring to the table, I can't afford not to bring you on. I know what you make for a living now, and I can only offer half of that. You have a family and little ones to feed. I'd like to have you on staff, but can you afford it?"

Before he could finish his sentence, I was jumping to respond!

"I can't lose! I believe God has told me to be in full-time ministry. If I can't make it, that means I was mistaken, and God didn't want me in full-time ministry after all. But if I'm supposed to be here, God will make a way."

God did make a way, and it was through my partner in life, love and calling, Michele. For two years she had lived her dream to be a full-time, stay-at-home mother. Yet when I presented the opportunity at Calvary, she did not hesitate to respond, "If God is opening that door for you, I'll go to work."

On February 1, 1991, I became a member of Calvary Assembly's pastoral staff. My "YES" to full-time ministry was finally fulfilled. My primary work was in outreach and pastoral care in the Decatur and Huntsville area. I was content, doing what I felt I was meant to do, even though I was not working with people suffering with addiction.

Michele and I had waited so many years for this day. Surely, I thought, I am hallucinating! No seminary education, a long-time drug addict, twice-divorced, I had disappointed so many people in so many ways, yet here I was, living my dream of ministering as a full-time pastor—and at one of the most dynamic churches in Alabama under a man I respected and loved. Once again, I could acknowledge the reality that God can take what little we have to give and, when we say "YES" with conviction to his vision for our lives, he can use us in ways we never imagined.

"God has given you potential, and it will be unleashed when your passion meets your purpose."

Bill

Ministers and Partners

It's time to talk about something that stands out to me in every chapter I have written about my road to the Promised Land. When I said "YES" with conviction to God's invitation to realize his vision for my life, it did not take long for me to understand just how important Michele's partnership was going to be if this journey was to be successful.

Michele helped accelerate my dream by giving up her own and saying, "I will follow yours and support you all the way." She did this in Cincinnati when it meant leaving her family, using up our savings and waiting for the call to Louisville. Her heart was as broken as mine when I was fired from the church there. Together we grieved, prayed, waited and wandered before making our way to Decatur and Calvary Assembly. She took the relocations, the packing and unpacking, the challenges, the big ideas and all our ups and downs in stride.

Michele has challenged me to pursue excellence in everything and to be the best I can be, and I have no doubt she will continue to do so. The truth is I have issues and bad habits, but she sharpens me. She has rescued me from embarrassing myself and assisted me when I did not

even realize I needed her help. I believe God brought Michele's patient and honest love into my life to help me avoid making many mistakes.

Psalm 91:9-12 (NIV) says: **"If you say, 'The Lord is my refuge,' and you make the Most High your dwelling, no harm will overtake you, no disaster will come near your tent.**

For he will command his angels concerning you to guard you in all your ways; they will lift you up in their hands, so that you will not strike your foot against a stone."

I am so thankful that God "commands his angels" to guard us in all our ways. In fact, I cannot imagine moving forward in my YES journey without them. I am equally thankful that he understands our need to have ministers and partners from the body of Christ—people he brings into our lives to walk with us, advise us and even guard us when necessary.

When I've been hurt, Michele has been right beside me to help me get up. She is my partner. Her devotion to me has reached deeply into my life through our relationship—not only as guardian and encourager, but also as someone to honestly and lovingly share with. I can only hope I've been an equal partner and minister to her. And I hope your journey is marked by the influence of partners and ministers, too.

Do not make the mistake of discounting the value of partnership in your own life journey. Remember those potholes, bumps, chasms and mountains we discussed earlier? You'll need someone alongside you when the road gets really rough. Ecclesiastes 4:9-12 (The Message) says it best:

> **It's better to have a partner than go it alone. Share the work, share the wealth.**
>
> **And if one falls down, the other helps, But if there's no one to help, tough!**
>
> **Two in a bed warm each other. Alone, you shiver all night.**
>
> **By yourself you're unprotected.**
>
> **With a friend you can face the worst. Can you round up a third?**
>
> **A three-stranded rope isn't easily snapped.**

Three strands, indeed. Besides Michele as my life partner and minister, God has brought other friends, ministers and partners into my life as well.

The Psalm 91 verses quoted earlier in this chapter show us God provides supernatural angels in our lives, but he also brings many people to minister to us, protect us and help move his work forward through us. Here are examples of this from my own life:

- Helena was the first to lead me to Christ through her actions and words. Without her I would never have started my journey in the first place.

- Without the pastor and his wife in Louisville who first took a chance on me, I would never have experienced the joy and contentment I found in the Market Street gutter with Jason. Despite the hardship and pain we experienced when I was fired, this couple set us on the road to The Foundry Ministries.

- George Sawyer took a step of faith in 1991 and offered me my first full-time job in ministry. Though he knew I was a twice-divorced, former drug addict without a seminary education, he took a chance that put me back on the road to my Promised Land. Pastor Sawyer mentored me during my years at Calvary Assembly, let me run with my ideas and challenged and guided me when I needed it most.

- And throughout my years as executive director of The Foundry Ministries, God has brought countless ministers, protectors and encouragers my way in the form of our staff and board, local pastors and even through consultants we have hired to advise us.

Your partner on the road may not be a husband or wife. It may be a close friend and confidante, a parent or sibling. It may be someone

who steps into your life and says "YES" to your journey when others say no.

Moses had a partner in Aaron—an older brother who became Moses' spokesperson and trusted assistant. Joshua and Caleb were encouragers for Moses, saying, "YES, God can!" to entering Canaan when others said an emphatic "No, we can't!" As a reward for their faith, Joshua and Caleb were the only Israelites of the first generation to enter into the Promised Land.

Remember that day when my car broke down between Dallas and Wharton, Texas? I didn't yet know Christ. I was very much alone and completely without support on the road. Today, no matter what happens, I can count on my partner Michele, and the many angels, partners and ministers God has surrounded me with to walk with me, support me and help protect me from making wrong decisions.

If you do not have a partner—if you have been trying to walk your journey alone—stop now and ask God to make partner and ministry connections in your life. Sharing the journey will make the road easier and the burdens lighter. Even better, the joy of reward doubles when there are two to enjoy it together!

In Exodus 4, God sent Aaron, Moses' older brother, to Moses to be a partner in the journey to the Promised Land. Throughout the books of

Exodus, Leviticus and Numbers, God often speaks to both men as though they are one. The brothers speak with one voice to Pharaoh and the Israelites, and God does miracles through both. They lead the people together; they discipline the people together; they perform sacrifices together. Moses and Aaron are true partners in every sense of the word.

But as close as Moses and Aaron were, some of Aaron's decisions were catastrophic for his family and for the nation of Israel. How could God give Moses such a partner?

The partnerships we make in life are made between human beings. No matter who your partners are in your journey to the Promised Land, it is essential that you realize the only perfect partner you will ever have is God and God alone.

God never talks about perfect human beings in his word because there are none. The partnerships you make will be with imperfect people— people like you and me!

God sends us the best, not the perfect.

You and your partner will disagree. You will challenge each other, disappoint each other, hurt each other, laugh, pray and plan with each other. You will need to forgive each other, too.

Remind yourself often that God is that perfect partner you said "YES"

to. He has set you on the course for your Promised Land and will walk beside you all the way.

"*I have learned that faith means trusting in advance what will only make sense in reverse.*"

Philip Yancey

Trust on the Road

Have you ever set out to do something that you knew would stretch you to the very limit? I am talking about something that takes hard work, lots of mental energy, determination and courage! Something like:

- Getting your college degree while working and caring for your family

- Adopting a child

- Building your own business

- Hiking the Appalachians

- Writing a book

- Running a marathon

- Overcoming a lifelong addiction

- Caring for an elderly parent

- Losing 25 or 50 or 100 pounds

- Parenting a troubled teen

Throughout the journey, you will find yourself experiencing all kinds of emotions, doubling back to correct mistakes, scratching your head as you figure out the next right thing to do, consulting with your family, your friends, your partner, your trusted advisors and praying as you've never prayed before!

As you near the end of your journey—take the finals, sign the papers, run your legs off, close the book—you may look back and ask yourself, "How did I ever manage to do that?"

The most valuable lesson I have learned throughout the years is that God's faithfulness is sure.

Since I gave my life to Christ back in 1979, I've been on one very long journey to the Promised Land called The Foundry Ministries. Yet I cannot discount the value of the shorter journeys from one "THAT moment" to the next "THAT moment." Each one has been an important part of the road, teaching me about myself and my God, and preparing me for the next step ahead.

The greatest day of my lifetime journey was the day I came to know Christ as my Lord and Savior. That was the day I began to trust that God would have my back in every circumstance. What a confidence builder that has been for me.

Hebrews 10:23 (NIV) puts it this way: "Let us hold unswervingly to the hope we profess, for he who promised is faithful."

No matter the circumstances you are walking through on your journey, he is faithful.

And in Lamentations 3:22-26 (NIV), the writer says that despite incredible hardship, it is:

> **Because of the Lord's great love we are not consumed, for his compassions never fail.**
>
> **They are new every morning; great is your faithfulness. I say to myself, "The Lord is my portion; therefore I will wait for him."**
>
> **The Lord is good to those whose hope is in him, to the one who seeks him; it is good to wait quietly for the salvation of the Lord.**

When I got saved, I decided to be confident in my partnership with God. Until he proved otherwise, I would accept unswervingly that he was trustworthy and I would believe with all my heart in his great faithfulness.

As our journey took off, Michele and I stepped out in faith again and again, and things started happening. Sometimes they happened when we didn't want them to. Sometimes we didn't like what was happening at all.

The important thing was that we were stepping out, confident that God would do through us what only he could do; and for that reason we could be confident he would see us through.

A great example of this is in the story of Abraham's own journey, and God's promise to make him the father of many nations. Paul explains it to the Romans in Romans 4:18-25 (The Message) this way:

> **Abraham was first named "father" and then became a father because he dared to trust God to do what only God could do: raise the dead to life, with a word make something out of nothing. When everything was hopeless, Abraham believed anyway, deciding to live not on the basis of what he saw he couldn't do but on what God said he would do. And so he was made father of a multitude of peoples. God himself said to him, "You're going to have a big family, Abraham!"**
>
> **Abraham didn't focus on his own impotence and say, "It's hopeless. This hundred-year-old body could never father a child." Nor did he survey Sarah's decades of infertility and give up. He didn't tiptoe around God's promise asking cautiously skeptical**

questions. He plunged into the promise and came up strong, ready for God, sure that God would make good on what he had said. That's why it is said, "Abraham was declared fit before God by trusting God to set him right."

But it's not just Abraham; it's also us! The same thing gets said about us when we embrace and believe the One who brought Jesus to life when the conditions were equally hopeless. The sacrificed Jesus made us fit for God, set us right with God.

I have already mentioned that the stories about David influenced my journey in a big way. His life is a great confidence and trust builder. No one knew better than David that God was trustworthy in the hardest of times, a refuge in times of oppression, a stronghold in times of trouble. When Saul wanted him dead, David was in survival mode every day. Yet, in Psalm 9:7-10 (NIV), in the midst of his hardship, David sings this song to the Lord:

The Lord reigns forever; he has established his throne for judgment.

He rules the world in righteousness and judges the peoples with equity.

The Lord is a refuge for the oppressed, a stronghold in times of trouble.

Those who know your name trust in you, for you, Lord, have never forsaken those who seek you.

You and I know his name. We can trust in him. He will never let you down as you move through your "YES" Journey with him.

"With what little that you have—the little God has given you—

you can change your family, your school, your community,

if you will let him be God and walk in faith to do what

he's called you to do."

Bill

Giants in the Land

David was confronted with a giant in the land. He trusted God and won.

When Moses was confronted by giants in the land, his story ended very differently. In Numbers 13:1-16, God invites Moses on a grand adventure—an exploration of the Promised Land. "Send some men to explore the land of Canaan ..." says the Lord, and Moses chooses a leader from each tribe to join the exploration team.

Moses gives the team its objective: evaluate the land, the people, their towns and the farmland, in verses 17-20. "Oh, and bring me back some grapes," he says.

The explorers travel for 40 days, covering miles of ground, visiting towns, sampling the soil, sizing up the people (they are huge!). Finally, they reach a valley where they gather samples of grapes, pomegranates and figs to take back to Moses, in verses 21-25.

Their report in verses 29-33 goes something like this: "The land is amazing. Milk and honey are abundant. And look at the size of this fruit! But if we're going to take the land, there are going to be problems. The

cities are like fortresses and the people are like giants. We felt like grass-hoppers around them, and we looked like grasshoppers to them."

In Numbers 14:1-5 the response from the Israelites is less than stellar, as usual. Instead of trusting God to pave the way into Canaan, they mope and grumble and consider heading back to Egypt again. And when Moses and Aaron hear all the complaining, they fall on their faces, literally.

The heroes in this story are Joshua and Caleb, the only two explorers who trust that God will empower his people to do the seemingly impossible: conquer the giants and take the land. They make their case in verses 6-9 (paraphrased):

"Wait a minute!" they beg. "God will lead us! He'll give us the land if he is pleased with us. Don't rebel and don't be afraid of the people. No matter how big they are, they are nothing when God is with us. We can do this!"

Rather than listen, the Israelites consider stoning Joshua and Caleb, and returning to Egypt. In verses 10-20, Moses begs the Lord not to kill the Israelites, reminding him that he is "slow to anger, abounding in love and forgiving sin and rebellion."

God honors his partnership with Moses, and lets the people live. Yet, he says in verse 23 (NIV), "Not one of them will ever see the land I promised

on oath to their ancestors. No one who has treated me with contempt will ever see it." In other words, none of them, including Moses and Aaron, would step foot into the Promised Land at the end of their journey.

Joshua and Caleb alone—the only men to put their trust and confidence in God—were allowed to enter the Promised Land 40 years later.

Once more for emphasis: **"No one who has treated me with contempt will ever see it," said the Lord.**

The Hebrew nation treated God with contempt when they refused to see past their fears, when they failed to put their trust in the one who had rescued them time and time again on their journey. This may be true for any one of us who show contempt for the Lord and his promises when we fail to put our trust in him on our own journeys to the Promised Land.

Listen, God knew there would be giants in the land of Canaan. He knew David would face a confrontation with Goliath. He knew I was going to face the giants of divorce, addiction, getting fired in Louisville and not knowing what my Promised Land would be like. And he knows that you will have to face a few giants on the journey, too.

Giants take away our confidence. But God says, "Don't lose confidence. When you do my will, I will take care of you."

In Exodus 23:20 (NIV), God tells his people, "See, I am sending an angel ahead of you to guard you along the way and to bring you to the place I have prepared." Proverbs 2:7-8 (NIV) reiterates God's promise of protection for us along our journey to the Promised Land he has prepared for us.

"He holds success in store for the upright, he is a shield to those whose walk is blameless, for he guards the course of the just and protects the way of his faithful ones."

On a "YES" journey, you are going where you have never gone before, doing what you have never done before. You are going into the unknown, and believe me, there will always be giants in the land. But you can be confident that when God calls you, he will protect you. He will not send you anywhere without providing for your needs. He will not send you into a land of giants only to let them beat you down. He is trustworthy and he will not fail you.

Your future, the outcome of each experience, your success in reaching the destination, depends on what you do in the defining moments that require courage, confidence and trust.

The "THAT moments" in your life, when you are facing your own giants, cannot be determined by emotional responses, knee-jerk reactions, refusal to see the truth, or by pride. These are the moments when your decisions

are critical, when the right or wrong choice affects your journey in the long-term, and it can either end the journey altogether or give you more confidence than ever for the road ahead.

I can't say it better than Peter, a disciple we can all identify with:

"Humble yourselves, therefore, under God's mighty hand, that he may lift you up in due time. Cast all your anxiety on him because he cares for you." I Peter 5:6-7 (NIV)

When you get hit with the unexpected, when things come at you out of left field, humble yourself and use these steps to keep things in perspective.

- Trust and acknowledge your Father and his love for you.

- Recognize his power.

- Remember what he has done for you.

- Cast your pain, your anger, your anxiety on his shoulders.

He knows the plan, and he is in control. **Get back on the road with confidence because he will lift you up and sustain you.**

"Walk by faith, not by sight.

Don't trust what you see, but what God says.

Without a deep consciousness of God you will not be able to face the roadblocks along the way."

Bill

Rounding the Bend to the Promised Land

More than three years had passed since Pastor Sawyer had invited me to join the pastoral staff at Calvary Assembly in Decatur. In those years, he'd provided an open field for me, allowing me to run in any direction as the Lord stirred up gifts in me I never knew I had. It was here that my passion, combined with my purpose, allowed me to experience the potential God had for my life. It just didn't get any better than this!

So how could I explain what I heard from the Lord one morning during my prayer time?

"Resign."

No. It was too bizarre ... as bizarre as any thought I'd had as a drug addict.

"Resign."

But why? Why on earth would I resign from a position of ultimate fulfillment? The thought was ludicrous!

"Resign."

Hmmm, apparently he was not going to let this go.

Questions flooded my mind. What was I going to do? Where was I going to go? How was I supposed to get there? And this question topped them all: How could I explain to my wife that I was going to resign, but had no idea why or where we were going?

We had children at home, responsibilities, debt and a mortgage! My anxiety grew as I imagined my conversation with Michele, but I heard nothing more from the Lord. I felt to some small degree what Abraham must have felt in Genesis chapters 21 and 22. He had waited years to receive the fulfillment of God's promise of a son, only to have God instruct him to take Isaac to the mountain and sacrifice him!

Of course, like Abraham, I did not know a ram was waiting in the bushes. As I fought through my concerns, I realized again that God had never let me down, even as he led our family into the unknown. He was trustworthy! If he was asking me to let go of what I thought of as my dream position, of course I would let go. It was time to step out in faith again and say "YES, Lord."

I gave notice in August 1994 and planned to leave my position six months later in February. Pastor Sawyer was gracious about the long months in between because he understood I had no idea what I was going

to do next. Though he wondered about my decision, he supported me just as he always had.

As I thought through my options, I considered offering leadership training to pastors and other people in ministry. Throughout the fall, I half-heartedly began compiling teaching materials. The time was growing short, and I still did not have a clue about my future. I prayed daily that God would clarify his direction sooner than later. In hindsight, I believe he was simply testing my faith before opening a series of doors that led to his ultimate plan for my life.

In December, the first door opened! A member of Calvary Assembly's board was also a board member at a nearby rescue mission. Knowing my situation, he called to tell me the mission had recently lost its executive director and needed an interim director while the board searched for new leadership. Could I stand in?

For the next month, I remained on the payroll at Calvary and divided my time between my pastoral duties there and the rescue mission. So many things needed immediate attention at the mission. Policies that had been set to protect the staff and clients were broken regularly. For example, one client simply lived in the mission's dayroom day after day, eating, smoking, sleeping and only leaving the room to go to the bathroom periodically.

Troubleshooting and putting things in order were right up my alley, and I dug right in, helping with facility improvements and developing policies and procedures that made the ministry more effective and safe for everyone.

The contentment and satisfaction I had known in Louisville resurfaced, and I found myself falling in love all over again with the hurting folks who needed to hear God's messages of hope and redemption.

I had been in my new job a few days when a friend from Calvary Assembly visited me at the mission. His concern for me showed in his eyes as he took in my surroundings.

"Bill, I am worried about you," he said. "You left a great church, a great pastor and a great future and look where you are now."

I could hardly contain my excitement as I shared with him that I was more content than I'd been in my life. The peace and happiness I felt confirmed what I knew about the value of saying "YES" to God, even when it didn't make sense. Though others couldn't see what Michele and I saw, though some folks questioned whether I was making the right decisions for my family, I knew that to be at peace, I had only to answer to God. Michele and I lived out Philippians 4:4-8 (NIV) as we followed what we knew to be the road God wanted us to travel:

Rejoice in the Lord always. I will say it: Rejoice! Let your gentleness be evident to all. The Lord is near. Do not be anxious about anything, but in every situation, by prayer and petition, with thanksgiving, present your requests to God. And the peace of God, which transcends all understanding, will guard your hearts and your minds in Christ Jesus.

We knew about the peace of God because we experienced it day after day. It really did guard us, warding off arrows of doubt and anxiety from people who loved us but did not understand our actions.

Isaiah 1:19 (NIV) assured us that, "If you are willing and obedient, you will eat the good things of the land." Our family was personally living out this scripture. God had taken care of us before and, once again, we were experiencing his supernatural protection and care.

Each day he told us, "I've got your back. I'll take care of you. Just make sure you do what you are supposed to do. I am in control. I have the power and authority to care for you when you can't. Just trust me and obey." We believed and obeyed with confidence, knowing he had consistently come through for us time and time again.

I experienced many "THAT moments" during my years at Calvary and now at the rescue mission. With each one, God broadened my expe-

rience, teaching me that, with his help, I could do things I had never done before—that when I was doing his will, he would equip me for whatever lay ahead. And in fact, I was driven to move forward regardless of how others felt, just as Peter and John were driven in Acts 4:18-20 (NIV), when they responded to the Sanhedrin's demands that they stop teaching in Jesus's name:

> **Then they called them in again and commanded them not to speak or teach at all in the name of Jesus. But Peter and John replied, "Which is right in God's eyes: to listen to you, or to him? You be the judges! As for us, we cannot help speaking about what we have seen and heard."**

Simply put, they said, "We gotta do what we gotta do." I felt the same way.

*"The only thing worse than being blind
is having sight but no vision."*

Helen Keller

Potholes in the Road … Again!

Strangely, three months into my interim service at the rescue mission, this first door closed as abruptly as it had opened. Once again, I just could not make sense of the situation.

A policy that is standard in every rescue mission I know of is that homeless guests cannot stay overnight in the shelter if they have been drinking. This mission had the same policy. In fact, a condition of my service as interim director was that I enforce this and other policies explicitly.

So when a taxi drove up to the mission's front door one evening, and John, one of our residents, got out and stumbled up the walk, I stopped him and said, "John, you're drinking. You can't even stand up straight. You can't stay here tonight."

The next day, I received a call from the board member who had originally arranged for John to join the mission's recovery program. When she asked why I hadn't let him in the building the night before, I explained the situation, confident that I'd done the right thing. But history seemed to repeat itself when I learned that she called an emergency board meeting that night, and the board voted to let me go.

Though this turn of events was disappointing, Michele and I had been here before, and we knew God had everything under control. The biggest problem was one of economics. My job at Calvary Assembly, as well as my paycheck, ended February 1. With the loss of my job at the mission, we had only Michele's paycheck to lean on, which was not enough to cover the bills or feed our family.

This problem was partially solved when God opened a second door. Right after I was fired from the mission in Decatur, I applied for the position of men's recovery program director at the Downtown Rescue Mission in Huntsville, Alabama (https://downtownrescuemission.org/). Though the job description included everything I loved to do, it paid only minimum wage. This was nowhere near enough to feed our family, even with the income Michele was bringing home.

I knew I wanted the job, but I would have to find an additional way to supplement our family income. As I assessed the problem, I realized that mowing lawns didn't take much experience, and I had an energetic 11-year-old son who could lend a hand at times. I decided I would start a lawn care business.

Amazingly, Michele again took my plans in stride, so I accepted the job at the Downtown Rescue Mission and put a lawn care ad in the local paper. Next I bought some used yard equipment, added a trailer to the back of my Chevy Lumina and waited for the calls to come in.

My career as a "lawn care specialist" was brief but colorful—literally. Customers who took a chance on me watched as I pulled my black Chevy Lumina into their driveways, followed by a bright red trailer loaded with an old green riding mower. I might not have looked terribly professional, but I did look very festive.

My education in professional lawn care started right away. As I pulled into my first customer's driveway, she caught sight of my Christmas-colored convoy through the front window and stuck around to watch the show.

I had known all along that hauling a lawn mower on a trailer attached to my Chevy wasn't the greatest idea in the world, but I couldn't afford to buy a truck, so I had to make do. I was alone on that first job, and getting the mower off the trailer was an acrobatic act requiring lots of shaking, jerking, balancing, jumping and even going airborne a time or two. At one point, as the mower blade wedged itself in the gap between the trailer and its door, I sat suspended briefly in midair. Thankfully and eventually, both the mower and I managed to land on the lawn uninjured, and I was able to get the job done. (Don't even ask how I got the mower back on the trailer!)

The lawn care jobs seldom went smoothly. My arsenal of used equipment just was not that reliable. Some days I would line up two or three jobs only to find out the mower wasn't going to cooperate or my used Weed Eater had bitten the dust.

Each morning I headed for the mission in Huntsville then rushed home at 4:30 to grab a bite to eat, change my clothes and go cut yards. Running from my job at the mission to my job as a grass cutter was physically taxing, but absolutely worth it. I was content because I knew I was doing what God wanted me to do. The peace of God was guarding my heart and mind as though I knew somehow that the Promised Land was waiting for me just around the bend. And as usual, Michele was right there with me all the way.

I had served as recovery program director for three months when the executive director resigned and, once again, I found myself filling in as interim director. I learned quickly that due to my lack of higher education and rescue mission experience, I would not be a candidate for the job, but my heart was still at peace.

You see, the months of rescue mission work in both Decatur and Huntsville were reawakening my once-shattered dream of working with addicted and homeless individuals, housing them, teaching them self-respect and building their self-esteem as they learned to be productive members of their communities.

As Michele and I reflected on our visit to Faith Farms and to our own experiences in Louisville, God resurrected the vision we left behind al-

most a decade ago. Convinced that we were finally nearing the Promised Land, we put our hands to the plow, filing the IRS forms for a 501(c)(3), forming a board of directors, raising money and aggressively looking for land big enough to contain our dream. We even had a name for our organization: the City of Hope.

Throughout the spring, summer and fall of 1995, Michele and I continued to plan. As my work at Huntsville drew to a close that summer, our passion and zeal collided with frustration. Though we were doing everything possible to build our dream, doors of opportunity would open only to shut tight at the last minute.

Sixteen months after I gave notice at Calvary Assembly—a time of growth, excitement, disappointment, frustration, passion and a lot of grass stains—Michele and I received a call that reminded us that God knew where the road would end all along.

December 11, 1995, we interviewed with the board members at Bessemer Rescue Mission (Bessemer, Alabama) and shared our vision for the City of Hope. The spirit was sweet. This board was very much in unity. On December 17, we received a phone call telling us that 100 percent of the board had voted for us to come. We went back two more times before accepting. Friday, December 22, we accepted.

The vision is the same and the potential is unlimited! All we could have hoped, dreamed and asked for has been answered. We are ready and excited … the kids are, too!"

from Michele's journal, December 23, 1995

Promised Land or Bust!

Bessemer, Alabama, is a city of around 27,000 inhabitants located in Jefferson County, just a few miles southwest of Birmingham. Established in 1887 as a mining and manufacturing town, Bessemer's economy was dependent on its iron and steel resources, which were exhausted by the 1980s. The town's Chamber of Commerce writes in its history: "The decline of mining and exodus of the steelmaking and railcar manufacturing industries resulted in the city facing an economic crisis in the early to mid-1980s; the percentage of unemployed workers reached into the mid 30s."

By the mid-90s, Bessemer's population had pulled itself through numerous economic downturns. The town was battered, but proud, with its government determined to find ways to improve the quality of life for its merchants and residents.

Though Michele and I had lived just 90 minutes away in Decatur, Alabama, neither of us had ever heard of Bessemer or its struggles until I received the call that brought us to the last leg of our journey.

When the phone rang in my office at the Downtown Rescue Mission in late fall, my family was wrapping up a year of starts and stops, and

more questions than answers. We were passionate about our desire to build the City of Hope, but as I mentioned earlier, even the best deals fell through, as though someone was working against us. In hindsight, we were living out Proverbs 19:21 (NIV): "Many are the plans in a man's heart but it is the Lord's purpose that will prevail."

The voice on the other end of the line was Bill Simpson's, a board member at the Bessemer Rescue Mission. He needed a reference for someone applying for the position of executive director there. Our conversation was pleasant and the Lord encouraged me to share my vision for the City of Hope.

A few days later, Bill called again. The position at Bessemer was not yet filled. Would I be interested in coming down for an interview? Because Michele and I already knew my days were numbered at the Downtown Rescue Mission, we were pretty excited about checking out this opportunity to see if it was a match for our vision.

On December 11, 1995, we traveled to Bessemer and toured the mission. As we walked through the building housing the men's emergency shelter, and the duplex next to it where a few homeless women and their children were housed, we tried to fit our very big vision for the City of Hope into their very limited spaces.

It just did not fit.

So, when the Bessemer Rescue Mission board offered me the position of executive director, I was grateful, but felt I had to say no, explaining that the vision for what God wanted to do was bigger than the capacity their facilities would allow. Undaunted, a board member mentioned that the First Alliance Church, a block away, could be for sale. "We're such a small mission, we never saw a need for it," he said, "but we'd consider buying it if the growth you envision comes true."

Unbelievable! A week later, I came back to tour the church and a partially completed two-story metal building beside it that had been intended as an education center before the church went into decline. I made my way through the entryway of the metal building and through the first floor, then headed up the stairs to the second story. Much of this floor remained unfinished, and I noted that it could easily be developed to meet our needs. My excitement grew as I looked down from a balcony to a gymnasium below. It was then that God spoke to me: "Bill, this is what you've waited for and what I created and prepared you for."

This was it. The Heintz family was going to pack up and move again. Only this time, we were moving to what we believed would be our final destination—the Promised Land we had waited for since 1987. A few days before Christmas, Michele and I headed back down to Bessemer for

one last talk with the board. If all went well, I would accept the position and begin serving as executive director just as the new year began.

Our excitement was tempered with Michele's growing anxiety about the effect another move would have on our kids. Decatur had been our home for several years. Now we were asking our children to adapt to a new town, a new school, a new church and new friends. Though she and the children were excited, she was also understandably concerned.

With each mile we drove, Michele's fears grew until she could hold back no longer and finally broke into tears. Searching for comfort, she turned to Isaiah 58:6-12 (NIV), a passage that had encouraged and motivated us for many years:

> **Is not this the kind of fasting I have chosen: to loose the chains of injustice and untie the cords of the yoke, to set the oppressed free and break every yoke?**
>
> **Is it not to share your food with the hungry and to provide the poor wanderer with shelter—when you see the naked, to clothe them, and not to turn away from your own flesh and blood?**
>
> **Then your light will break forth like the dawn, and your healing will quickly appear; then your**

righteousness will go before you, and the glory of the Lord will be your rear guard.

Then you will call, and the Lord will answer; you will cry for help, and he will say: Here am I.

If you do away with the yoke of oppression, with the pointing finger and malicious talk, and if you spend yourselves in behalf of the hungry and satisfy the needs of the oppressed, then your light will rise in the darkness, and your night will become like the noonday.

The Lord will guide you always; he will satisfy your needs in a sun-scorched land and will strengthen your frame.

You will be like a well-watered garden, like a spring whose waters never fail.

Your people will rebuild the ancient ruins and will raise up the age-old foundations; you will be called Repairer of Broken Walls, Restorer of Streets with Dwellings.

What an incredible answer to any concerns we felt about this move. Not only was this a mandate for the ministry we were preparing to pioneer, but also promise after promise of how God would care for our family as we stepped out in faith and journeyed to this new land. If we would do what he told us to do, he would take care of our kids and every other concern we had. He would answer when we called. He would satisfy our needs. He would strengthen and enlighten us.

He would be our rearguard, protecting our children from harm!

With our anxieties put to rest, Michele and I could concentrate even more fully on the mandate in Isaiah 58. The Message's translation of verse 12 really connected with me because of my own life experiences before and after I came to know Christ:

> **You'll use the old rubble of past lives to build anew, rebuild the foundations from out of your past. You'll be known as those who can fix anything, restore old ruins, rebuild and renovate, make the community livable again.**

Our new ministry would offer a process through which people, like me, who had been broken, could experience real transformation. It would take the rubble of their lives and through God's grace and power, restore, rebuild and renovate them!

As we pulled into the parking lot at the Bessemer Rescue Mission, Michele and I could agree together that we were ready to take on this new

adventure and give it our all. Within the hour, Bessemer Rescue Mission had a new executive director, his enthusiastic wife and a new vision for its future.

On January 1, 1996, as I drove in for my first day of work, I surveyed the blocks around the mission as plans for the ministry and the community that would support it flooded my mind. I was ready to face the giants that would come my way, and I could not wait to get started.

I've always admired Bill's wisdom, and I leaned on it greatly as I grew as a wife, mother and Christian. In addition to his wisdom, I began to recognize early in our marriage that one of his spiritual gifts was faith. And not just a basic level of faith, I believe Bill has an unusually great measure of faith. Looking back, I know now you can't be a visionary without it!

Bill is a fearless man of faith! Though there was a lot of adversity and many naysayers in our early years of ministry,

Bill's faith never waivered.

Though the conception of the vision in 1987, to its fruition in 1996, took almost a decade,

Bill's faith never waivered.

His great faith simply allowed him to believe that if God said to do it, nothing and no one could stop it.

Bill's 'faith eyes' see the impossible. When our first bookkeeper said we'd never make it, and the ministry doors would be closed,

Bill knew God would provide.

His faith never waivered.

A friend of the ministry once labeled Bill a "visionary out of control." Bill received that as a compliment. If he could dream it, he believed God could do it. Bill "saw" The Foundry in 1987, and he never let go of the vision. Why?

Because his faith never waivered.

Michele

I'm Not Going Anywhere

Ready. Set. Whoa … whoa … whoa!

As the new executive director of the Bessemer Rescue Mission, I was barely out of the starting gate when the first potholes and barriers emerged. A few days into my new position, I prepared for a board meeting where I would roll out plans for the recovery program and its job training component. I approached the meeting with confidence, believing the board would respond with enthusiasm and support. But before I could speak, the chairman of the board made a motion to "Dismiss Bill Heintz."

I survived that meeting, only to learn a few days later that a second meeting had been called by the chairman with the same agenda item. Then a third. At this point, one sympathetic board member gently suggested, "Bill, maybe it would be better if you just went back to Decatur. This doesn't seem to be working out."

Actually, this proposition seemed somewhat attractive after what I had been through so far. We still had not moved our family so I was commuting more than 90 miles each way to work every day, only to be regularly met with negativity and skepticism. It was frustrating and wearing on my

nerves. Yet I knew God had told me to come to Bessemer and leaving was not an option.

"God brought me here," I said. "To tell you the truth, my flesh would love for me to quit, but until God tells me to go or you fire me, I'm not going anywhere."

For the third time, the board rejected the motion to "Dismiss Bill Heintz." When a fourth meeting was called a few days later with the same motion on the table, the board dismissed the chairman!

But more trouble was brewing in Bessemer. Throughout the church community, the buzz was that there was a new director at the rescue mission and he was turning the place upside down. I was even compared to the cult leader Jim Jones! Finally, the president of the local Baptist Association agreed to come for a visit and find out for himself what I was doing. During our time together, I sensed his openness to hear about the vision for the City of Hope. As I explained and we prayed together, he began to see the new vision and we parted friends.

The toughest folks to convince were the 18 addicted and unemployed men who had been staying at the mission every night before I became executive director. After accepting the position in December, I'd come down during an evening meal when I was sure I would catch most of them, and explained that in addition to the mission providing emergency relief

124

services to the community, the Bessemer Rescue Mission would become a place of recovery and accountability for individuals who wanted to overcome addictions and become productive members of the community. All 18 men chose to leave the mission for greener (easier) pastures.

As naysayers came and went, I plowed forward knowing I had said "YES, Lord" to this particular Promised Land, and I was going to do what God had told me to do. To some, I'm sure I looked like a visionary out of control! To others, I looked like I had bitten off more than I could chew.

My service at Bessemer Rescue Mission began with two staff members—Michele and me—and seven recovery program participants who'd followed us to Bessemer from the Downtown Rescue Mission.

We were a tiny army up against several giants:

- facilities that needed repair,

- a recovery program to be developed,

- fundraising to support the ministry

- and, of course, the skepticism we faced so often

But, I had "the staff of God" in my hand and my wife Michele as an advisor, strategic thinker and prayer partner. We could do this thing.

Our fledgling ministry took off, and over the next few weeks we all worked together cleaning, painting and brightening the interior of the mission just as we were brightening the vision for its future!

One morning, I stood under the awning at the front of the mission, just taking in the scene around me when one of our program participants walked up to me and asked, "Pastor Bill, what do you see?" I had been thinking of all the opportunities for growth, the skills our program participants were sharing with us, the vision that was already taking shape as I responded with, "What God wants to do, I can't even comprehend."

That day, as the work went on all around me, as the endless possibilities stretched out before me, I realized that when you know God is the author of your vision, you can believe in the impossible and the invisible. He will give you the people and the tools to make it happen, and together, you'll go places you could never go alone.

I realized that arriving in your Promised Land is just the beginning of a new adventure!

Watch out for stop signs on your journey.

Someone asked if we ever thought about giving up. No. We were tenacious, which means "not easily stopped."

Ministry life is sure to bring challenges and victories, hard work and fulfillment, grief and joy. Were there days of weariness? You bet. Financial challenges? Of course! Naysayers? Always. Tempted to quit? Never.

Why?

The moment you discover why you were born, what your purpose on earth is, when God's purpose and your YES intersect, there is an undeniable driving force within you that is not satisfied unless you are fulfilling God's purpose in your life.

The road on your journey may be filled with unexpected stops, detours, and various difficulties and challenges. Doing life according to God's purpose doesn't exempt you from bumps, gravel, or potholes on your road. You know you are called when, despite treacherous road conditions, you have peace and you know you are not alone. There is no stopping and no turning back. Your navigator, the Holy Spirit, is leading you to your Promised Land.

If you are miserable in life, ask God if you are running from or denying your God-given purpose.

Michele

Endure, Wait and Trust

This adventurous road to the Promised Land is full of turns and twists, hills and valleys. As I've said before, I'm so thankful God doesn't show us these things as we begin the journey because it isn't until he has "shown up" for us during the hard times that we really understand we can and must endure.

Though my passion for full-time ministry dominated my thinking soon after I came to know Christ in 1980, it wasn't until 1991 that I began to fully live out that passion. I didn't know God had a training schedule in mind—one that would get me in shape for fulfilling his dream for my life. God knew I could not have handled jumping into full-time ministry right away. In retrospect, I am thankful he prepared me first by teaching me the value of endurance.

One Bible promise that helped me to be patient on the journey was Isaiah 40:31 (KJV): "But they that wait upon the Lord shall renew their strength; they shall mount up with wings as eagles; they shall run, and not be weary; and they shall walk, and not faint."

Early on in our adventure in Bessemer, Michele and I attended our first Association of Gospel Rescue Missions (AGRM) convention. This organization (www.agrm.org) connects more than 300 gospel rescue missions of every size and shape throughout the United States, and we knew we'd find like-minded, experienced "mission workers" there who could help guide and encourage us, which they have without fail. Some of the executive directors we met led missions with hundreds of full-time employees. Their ministries included all the things we'd dreamed of for years, but didn't have now.

I came back from that convention inspired but overwhelmed. I knew God wanted to do great things in Bessemer, but our ministry seemed so little in comparison to older, more established, missions around the country. Thankfully, I could look back down the road we'd traveled and remember how he'd grown each ministry we'd been involved with. With those wonderful memories in mind, I knew we'd simply need to bide our time, endure, and watch as he fulfilled his dream for The Foundry.

Though I make it sound like it was easy to wait, I often cried out to God on my journey, "When, God, when?!" Thankfully, my partner, Michele, wisely responded to my frustration time after time, saying, "Bill, I'll tell you when God is going to do it—when he decides it's time."

Hebrews 10:23 (NIV) says, "Let us hold unswervingly to the hope that we profess, for he who promised is faithful." Understanding the power of this promise will save you a lot of sleepless nights worrying about

things you do not have the power on your own to accomplish. Just know this: **God *will* fulfill the dreams he gives you.** Worrying won't make them happen any faster, so say "YES, Lord" to his timing when you say "YES, Lord" to the journey!

"Isn't it funny how day by day nothing changes,

but when you look back, everything is different..."

C.S. Lewis, "Prince Caspian"

Choosing to Change

When Michele and I look back across our years together, one thing has been consistent on our journey to the Promise Land: our need to accept and value change. Thankfully, the presence and purpose of God through each change he has asked us to make has been even more consistent.

I think we've been pretty good at rolling with the punches. At the same time, there have been times when one or both of us have been a little resistant, when "change now" seemed too soon, too hard or just too big a surprise. For example:

- To say that leaving the ministry behind in Louisville was really hard would be an enormous understatement.

- Taking our kids away from the familiar in Decatur brought about many questions and tears.

These experiences and so many others required us to trust in the consistent care of God as we moved from one way of living, thinking and doing to another. And I'm so glad we did!

Living through decades of changing circumstances has given me some insight into why human beings find it so hard to handle change at

times—and why it's so critical to accept and even welcome change. Here's the first thing you have to know: You will encounter change and you will cause change regularly on your "YES" journey. It is inevitable, but with God at the controls you can move forward, even when it hurts.

Listen to Peter's message to the Jewish Christians fleeing persecution, and to believers today in I Peter 4:1-2 (The Message):

> **Since Jesus went through everything you're going through and more, learn to think like him. Think of your sufferings as a weaning from that old sinful habit of always expecting to get your own way. Then you'll be able to live out your days free to pursue what God wants instead of being tyrannized by what you want.**

When we "think like Jesus" and focus on what God wants rather than our own way, we have the freedom to pursue (run toward) change.

But sometimes we are not willing to broaden our thinking. We get stuck on being stubborn. The change God is asking us to make might be too much to comprehend. Run toward it? No way! It looks like hard work. It might even mean turning away from the "way we've done it for years."

It might require all of that. **But being willing to change is so important that it comes up again and again in the New Testament.**

Paul tells the Christians in Rome one of the most basic principles of walking out the Christian life: "Do not conform to the pattern of this world, but be transformed by the renewing of your mind. Then you will be able to test and approve what God's will is—his good, pleasing and perfect will." Romans 12:2 (NIV)

I like the way the New Living Translation says it, too:

> **"Don't copy the behavior and customs of this world but let God transform you into a new person by changing the way you think. Then you will learn to know God's will for you, which is good and pleasing and perfect."**

In the ministry of recovery, the "renewing of the mind" is crucial. Recovery requires an addicted person to change from an old mindset to a new mindset. To change your addictive behavior, you first have to change the way you think. Instead of, "I need to get high," you need to think, "I don't want to get high." You have to want to change. You have to be willing to change the way you think.

That's not easy for an individual who has been thinking for years: "I am born an addict and I will die an addict." But once the addict changes the way he or she thinks and decides "Maybe I can do this," the real process of transformation can begin.

When I change my thinking, I give myself permission to change what I believe about myself, about others, about life, about learning new things. The opportunities are limitless. **So it's important to make sure my beliefs measure up to the truths of God.** Philippians 4:8 (NIV) gives me direction on what to think about: "Finally, brothers and sisters, whatever is true, whatever is noble, whatever is right, whatever is pure, whatever is lovely, whatever is admirable—if anything is excellent or praiseworthy— think about such things."

Changing what you think and what you believe can have an enormous impact on the world around you.

On July 20, 1969, Buzz Aldrin and Neil Armstrong made history as the first men to land on the moon, which was something no one would have believed possible in 1903 when the Wright Brothers took to the air in a small propeller-driven plane at Kitty Hawk. Apparently, at some point between 1903 and 1969, someone looked at the moon and said to himself, "I bet we could get up there if we really tried, but we'll need to use something more powerful than a propeller to do it."

Those thoughts evolved into beliefs that changed the way scientists looked at space travel and at the universe. In fact, the changes that took us from propellers to rocketing to the moon have affected the way we travel, learn and communicate; they have even affected the foods we eat!

All because someone opened his mind and altered his beliefs.

In the 1990s, when I realized that computers were here to stay and would change everything about the way the world communicated, my thinking went from, "YES, I'm willing to open my mind to technology," to "I believe technology will help make The Foundry successful," to "I expect our staff to learn and use technology to bring about the best possible results."

I no longer needed convincing. Instead, I began focusing on hiring people who could take us as far as we could go using the Internet, social media, data processing and other technological resources. I expect The Foundry to continue to learn and grow with each new resource available.

Expectancy is something Paul was really familiar with. In his letter to the Romans, he said:

> **There's more to come. We continue to shout our praise even when we're hemmed in with troubles, because we know how troubles can develop passionate patience in us, and how that patience in turn forges the tempered steel of virtue, keeping us alert for whatever God will do next. In alert expectancy such as this, we're never left feeling shortchanged. Quite the contrary—we can't round up enough containers**

to hold everything God generously pours into our lives through the Holy Spirit. Romans 5:3-5 (The Message)

When you have positive expectations, you create a stir of expectancy and excitement in your environment.

It's contagious! What happened after Aldrin and Armstrong walked on the moon? It wasn't long before someone said, "Now let's try for Mars!"

Expectancy says, "There's more to come so stay alert! Let's see what God does next!" Expectancy drives you forward, gives you confidence to take that next important step and the one after that.

When I became the executive director of the Bessemer Rescue Mission in 1996, I started talking about the new things we would do, things that had never been done there before. I know I took a lot of people by surprise, and some folks just were not sold on the vision God had given me for the mission's future at all. They liked the old way and so I became a threat.

But when people began to see what was happening at the mission, they began to embrace the changes we were making. They began to believe the new ways could work. And they began to expect better results!

Of course, this process didn't happen overnight, but eventually folks who had earlier questioned the changes we were making began to cheer us on. As they learned to anticipate the next improvement and the next transformed life, they changed their attitudes, too.

A positive attitude can create a great environment for change and success. Imagine where you started when this whole "change thing" came up, then compare it with the way a positive attitude allows you to think and communicate:

- "I don't see it that way" becomes "Why didn't I see this before?"

- "We're doing it the old way" becomes "Let's try something new!"

- "You want me to do what?" becomes "How can we get this done?"

- "It's not my job" becomes "I'll do whatever it takes!"

- "I don't like what I'm seeing" becomes "I can't wait to see what happens next."

You have seen the power of change. You have experienced it firsthand. You discovered that the way things were can become the way things are, and that the way they can be in the future is worth pursuing. As your attitude reaches out to breathe life into your expectations, your behavior naturally gets into the race, too.

I have noticed something about people who resist change: they cycle around in a pattern of behavior with the same results again and again:

- the drug addict remains addicted to drugs

- the person who hates his job continues to complain

- the spendthrift remains in debt

- the person with the outdated GPS system keeps getting lost

One of my favorite quotes, often attributed to baseball Hall-of-Famer Yogi Berra, is this: "Nothing changes if nothing changes." But when a Christ-follower accepts the idea of change and believes in its value, expects good things and is motivated to make them happen, that person's behavior gets into the act and it affects everyone around them. Now that's when things really begin to happen!

Recently, I announced that The Foundry's annual theme would be "Discover Your Potential" based on Ephesians 1:11-12 (The Message):

It's in Christ that we find out who we are and what we are living for. Long before we first heard of Christ and got our hopes up, he had his eye on us, had designs on us for glorious living, part of the overall purpose he is working out in everything and everyone.

Men and women come to The Foundry every day without purpose but with all kinds of gifts and talents locked away because of their addictions. Right away, we talk to them about their skills and give them an opportunity

to contribute somewhere on our campuses or in our enterprises. Imagine if we did not require them to change their behavior before they got to work.

I don't know about you, but I don't want a mechanic, no matter how talented he is, to tamper with the engine of my car if he is high on drugs. However, if his behavior changes, if he stops using drugs and takes recovery seriously so that his hands are steady, and his mind can work clearly, then his job performance improves 100 percent. Now, I'm going to give him an opportunity to work on a donated car that we are refurbishing and selling. I'm going to tell others, "We have a great mechanic at The Foundry! You need to come buy one of the cars he's worked on!"

I've encountered this in my own YES journey and as a leader. As I've broadened my thinking, accepted new ideas, and taken risks in my personal and professional life, I've been able to grow in ways I couldn't have if I'd been unwilling to change. **As my performance as a person, leader and employer has improved, our organization has improved, too.**

When I see that those improvements have resulted because my performance has changed for the better, I just want to keep getting better and better. I want to see how far I can go.

The Foundry is all about reshaped lives.

We believe firmly that, through a relationship with Jesus Christ, anyone has the potential to go places they never thought they could go and do things they never thought they could do.

I love Jesus, and my Christian walk has taken me on a journey I would never have dared to dream of. You cannot convince me there is a better way to live, because when you trust in God and follow his vision, there is no end to what he will do in your life.

Here is the simple message we share with our program participants. "Therefore, if anyone is in Christ, the new creation has come: The old has gone, the new is here!" II Corinthians 5:17 (NIV) When you change what you believe, think and do, you change your life. You have broken free of trends, traditions and "the old ways" to make room for invention, creativity and growth. You have reached the moon and have opened up a door to go to Mars!

In my two-decade career in this Promised Land, I've made a lot of changes, taken a lot of risks, made a lot of progress. We did not do things in 2016 the same way we did in 1996. And we won't do things in the years to come the way we do them today.

Progress requires change. If you want progress, if you want a life and a ministry that is always moving forward, doing new things and then do-ing them even better, embrace change, get to know people who challenge

your thinking, share with and hire people who bring new ideas to the table, step out on a limb and take a calculated risk.

Be someone who attracts phenomenal people and expect them to do things differently. Challenge them to change the status quo instead of hindering their ideas.

Let God do His work of transformation in you, in those you serve in leadership and in your work and world.

"I am delirious with contentment.

And the best thing is, I wasn't qualified
for what I do in my Promised Land
each day, but God took what little I
could give and anointed it!

What's my 'little'?

It's so little I can't even tell you."

Bill

Bigger Vision

As I may have mentioned a few times by now, it's amazing that a ministry like The Foundry has become what it is with me at the helm. I knew I had the vision, and I knew God had chosen me to lead, but I also knew the dream was far bigger than me. As the ministry grew, and it did right from the beginning, I believed that God would send me the people I needed to build a team with passion, purpose and a whole lot of potential.

Within a few months, Bessemer Rescue Mission was well over its 18-bed capacity. People were sleeping in the hallways, the dining hall, the chapel—anywhere we could put a mattress. It was the mission version of "If you build it, they will come." Apparently, God knew a lot of people who needed a recovery program with a work component, and he wasn't going to let little things like a lack of staff, space or money get in the way.

All of the homeless men and women coming to the mission were addicted to drugs or alcohol, and many had long been unemployed, but they were talented, too. A hair stylist, a landscaper, a mechanic, a salesperson, a decorator, a carpenter—our program participants had a huge variety of skills lying dormant after years of addiction, just waiting to be used again. As we welcomed them into the recovery program and assessed

their needs and gifts, we could clearly see how God could use each person uniquely as he or she left the addiction behind and traded it for self-respect, productivity and an opportunity to be a benefit to the community.

Because our staff was so small, we really needed the skills our residents brought to the table. Often, while they were still in our program, the program participants assisted with everything from cooking and cleaning to all kinds of office work. As you can imagine, this was risky business at times, but we also saw many of our residents bloom as they realized they were valued and needed in our growing ministry.

Just a year after coming to the mission, we had grown to the extent that it was time to purchase the First Alliance Church building I had toured before accepting the position in Bessemer. When I approached the church's pastor and told him the mission wanted to buy it, he said, "Lots of people have said that, but they've never come through." This made perfect sense to me, and I explained, "That's because you were trying to sell my church to somebody else!"

Some on our board and staff were skeptical, too.

When I told our board and bookkeeper it was time to buy the church and increase our bed capacity, they were short on enthusiasm and long on questions. Finally, they asked me to produce a projected budget for the coming year before they made a decision.

I turned in a budget of $490,000, much of which would cover the cost of the church. The response was less than positive and the conversation went something like this:

Them: "You barely made your first-year budget of $220,000. How do you propose to get the other $270,000?"

Me: "I don't have a clue."

Them: "This seems too risky and we don't know what kind of local support we will get. If we try this, we could end up running the mission into the ground."

Me: "I don't know anything about local support, but I do know God. He told us to buy the building and how he chooses to accomplish that is up to him."

It was a battle between common sense and faith.

Frankly, the board had a lot of good reasons not to buy that building but, praise God, after a lot of consideration and prayer, they voted to take a step of faith.

With confidence, we approached a local bank for a $225,000 loan, but were quickly turned down. Then a couple on our board decided to take their own leap of faith and vouch for the mission and for me. The building was ours!

This first miracle was followed by many more. As our need to increase capacity grew, so did the need for more real estate, along with the need for more funding. God knew that my desire to grow the vision and take great leaps of faith would have to be counter-balanced with the wisdom of men and women I could respect and trust—people who would ask hard questions and continue to stabilize the ministry in its growth.

As the years passed, our board added accountants, lawyers and other business people to its ranks. "I don't have a clue, but God does" no longer satisfied their questions. I had to have real answers. When the budget looked more red than black, "It'll work out" just did not satisfy these folks. There were times when approaching board meetings was downright intimidating for me, but I knew God was using these tough new ministry partners to teach and guide me, and to provide the knowledge I knew all too well I did not possess at the time.

As our outreach, buildings and board expanded and grew, we also found the need to grow our staff. Leadership in my Promised Land has meant finding people with core competencies that can get the job done. The most important factor in hiring for The Foundry has been the ability to connect with their heart for ministry. All the competencies in the world do not make a fit for the ministry. If a potential employee's heart, ideals and drive match with our mission of changing lives, and they are willing

to learn, adapt and apply their competencies along with their heart, that makes a good fit for us.

The right attitude can determine your success in your personal Promised Land journey and the success of your ministry, relationships, business and family.

Often, a right attitude is about serving and putting others before yourself and moving beyond your own comfort zone.

Facing the giants, obstacles and hurdles in your Promised Land with the right attitude can widen, broaden and deepen your vision. This right attitude includes faithfully letting God put people and circumstances in place on your behalf. If it is his will, his way and his timing, he will make it happen.

*"We must not become dry, brittle, and inflexible.
And we must endeavor to bounce back,
no matter how we may feel."*

John Maxwell, "Beyond Talent"

Big Changes

Over the past 20 years, The Foundry has grown a bit. Well, that's an understatement when you compare the ministry we took on in 1996 to what it is today. Though I was obviously here when it happened, the increase in the number of our program participants, and the buildings and budget these require, still takes my breath away. It is mind boggling. What is really exciting is that our growth translates into more lives touched, changed and reshaped.

Along with the changes to our growth and impact over the last 20 years, we have also changed our name twice.

During the time I was ministering at the mission in Decatur, and later at the Downtown Rescue Mission in Huntsville, Michele and I began to dream of our own ministry, built from scratch and called the City of Hope.

Two years after I became the executive director of Bessemer Rescue Mission, I was really excited that the name of the mission was officially changed to the City of Hope. But in 2004, I found out that the name had been nationally trademarked many years earlier.

I loved the name City of Hope but, since it was already being used, I reluctantly agreed to hire a professional firm to help us choose the best name for the ministry.

The hand of God has always been on and in what is now called The Foundry Ministries. He even orchestrated our new name—one I initially did not like at all.

During our first meeting with one of the partners from the firm we hired, I expressed my sadness at the name change. In response, he tried to educate me on what an organization's name should say.

He said, "If you have the proper name, it will tell people three things: who you are, what you do, and where you are." He then went on to tell me that the name "City of Hope" did none of those things. This first conversation kind of rubbed me the wrong way, but I decided to let him try and help us anyway.

His next visit was intended to find out who we were and what we did. He showed up at 7 a.m. to attend the first recovery class of the day and left at 8:30 p.m. following our weekly chapel service. Overwhelmed, he admitted he hadn't realized how versatile we were and how much we had to offer. He would take the information he had gathered and get back to us soon.

A couple weeks later, he came back and told us he had the perfect name—one that had all three identifiers.

First he showed us a draft of the logo: it was a picture of a man beating an object with a hammer. In fact, it looked like a man beating another man over the head! I was pretty frustrated as I thought to myself: "You spent two weeks coming up with this idea? You want us to advertise that our ministries work by beating people over the head?"

Then he turned to the next page of his flip chart and showed us the name: The Foundry. I was steaming now! "What kind of spiritual name is this?" I thought. "Surely, it could have the word 'hope' or 'God' or something in it!"

While I was busy seething away, Michele and Leslie, our then development director, were grinning up a storm. They understood what a foundry was and loved the name. I just did not get it. The whole thing was driving me crazy!

Finally, he put up the tagline: "Where Lives Are Reshaped by the Hands of God." I was beside myself and it showed.

By this time, the guy could tell I was very upset. "If you don't like it, I can go back and come up with something else," he said, "but nothing will be this good." Then he packed his things and left.

I let the whole issue go for a week or so until Leslie called me into her office one morning to talk. We were moving our thrift store to its new 90,000 square-foot location, and she needed to order signage. "Have you made up your mind?" she wanted to know. When I told her I was still skeptical about the name, she said, "You, as our visionary and leader, need to decide what to go with. I'm asking God to make it undeniably clear to you if The Foundry is the name intended for this ministry."

I left that day feeling trapped. Everyone else loved the name, but I just could not get on board.

The next morning, the father of a very troubled young man came to my office to talk. In his frustration, he said, "Until God takes my son, places him on the anvil and uses the hammer to reshape him, my son will not change!"

I knew right then the name would be "The Foundry."

I was completely convinced when I visited a foundry in Bessemer the following day and saw the process for myself. I was totally blown away! I realized that the purpose of a foundry is to take something that's been discarded and make it useful again. As I watched a giant magnet drop into a pile of scrap metal and pick up pieces of rubble, I thought, "That's the Holy Spirit drawing someone out of addiction and hopelessness." Then I saw the rubble being put into a fire to be purified before it

154

was molded into something new. Wow! In our ministry, God takes lives deemed useless and makes them new. At that point, everything fell into place and I walked away from my visit convinced that our new name was to be "The Foundry."

The process that someone goes through to get free from brokenness and addiction and move toward their personal Promised Land is much like the transformation that metal goes through in a foundry. The Foundry Ministries uses the WAY path to move program participants through this process, which we refer to as The Foundry Way™.

The Foundry Way™ starts with the foundation of Yield to God's Leadership, then moves to Align with God's Purpose and, finally, culminates with Work to Make a Difference. Yield, Align and Work form an acrostic from the bottom up to spell WAY.

3. Work to Make a Difference

2. Align with God's Purpose

1. Yield to God's Leadership

The verses below illustrate the biblical basis for some of the ideas of The Foundry Way™ and show the process I went through on my personal Promised Land journey and what you must also go through to get to yours.

Yield to God's Leadership

Come to me, all you who are weary and burdened, and I will give you rest. Take my yoke upon you and learn from me, for I am gentle and humble in heart, and you will find rest for your souls. For my yoke is easy and my burden is light. Matthew 11:28-30 (NIV)

"For my thoughts are not your thoughts, neither are your ways my ways," declares the Lord. "As the heavens are higher than the earth, so are my ways higher than your ways and my thoughts than your thoughts." Isaiah 55:8-9 (NIV)

Align with God's Purpose

Don't copy the behavior and customs of this world, but let God transform you into a new person by changing the way you think. Then you will learn to know God's will for you, which is good and pleasing and perfect. Romans 12:2 (NLT)

"For I know the plans I have for you," declares the Lord, "plans to prosper you and not to harm you, plans to give you hope and a future." Jeremiah 29:11 (NIV)

Work to Make a Difference

> **... and if you spend yourselves in behalf of the hungry and satisfy the needs of the oppressed, then your light will rise in the darkness, and your night will become like the noonday.** Isaiah 58:10 (NIV)

"'Twant me, 'twas the Lord.
I always told him, 'I trust to you.
I don't know where to go or what to do,
  but I expect you to lead me,'
and he always did."

Harriet Tubman

The Long Haul

Along with the adventure your "YES" Journey has in store, there may be many days where you feel that you are plodding along, when no exciting miracles are happening and there are no milestones immediately ahead. What happens in those quiet or boring times? When you're pushing papers around your desk, there's nothing new on the horizon and you want to go home early because there's nothing interesting to do in your personal Promised Land?

For someone like me, these "ordinary days" are a bigger struggle than the times I have to face big challenges. With the big things, you automatically know you have to have faith and be on your toes. When you are going through the everyday stuff, keeping your eyes on the vision can be a challenge.

Have you ever needed to lose weight?

The first week might get you excited as you lose a few pounds fast. Then as the weeks pass, the whole process becomes a grind. You step on the scales, and the reward is so little that it's hard to stay on track. But down the road, because you stuck it out for the long haul, you suddenly

see the results of the little things you did day in and day out. You are healthier and stronger. You feel more confident in yourself and in your ability to do what needs to be done. That's when you know the daily grind is worth it.

It's not easy to stay on course when there is no big, exciting goal ahead. Strangely, it's during those times that you really have to focus and persevere. You have to be watchful during those "business as usual" days, those times your adrenaline is not going full force because it's just another day.

When you are not as vigilant as you should be, small things can go unnoticed. Things can pile up and become big problems later: staff conflicts that have been allowed to fester; strategic weaknesses that get pushed to the back burner; budgetary problems that everyone has been happy to ignore because something more exciting was going on.

Use those not-so-exciting times to solve the small stuff. Dealing with them now will help you avoid future hardships and make the "big days" that much better.

Colossians 1:9-12 (The Message) says this:

> **Be assured that from the first day we heard of you,**
> **we haven't stopped praying for you, asking God to**

give you wise minds and spirits attuned to his will, and so acquire a thorough understanding of the ways in which God works. We pray that you'll live well for the Master, making him proud of you as you work hard in his orchard. As you learn more and more how God works, you will learn how to do your work. We pray that you'll have the strength to stick it out over the long haul—not the grim strength of gritting your teeth but the glory-strength God gives. It is strength that endures the unendurable and spills over into joy, thanking the Father who makes us strong enough to take part in everything bright and beautiful that he has for us.

Use these days to get close to your Heavenly Father, asking for a wise mind and spirit, and building endurance so you can stick it out over the long haul.

During the days when you feel nothing but the grind of day-to-day duties, seek out the things that have been neglected while you were busy pursuing the exciting challenges that came with the vision. Let him build your strength and the strength of your ministry for the big things ahead.

Being in your Promised Land is not always about the exciting stuff.

Being in your Promised Land is also about the everyday stuff that keeps you sharp: reading, praying, planning, observing and building alongside your brothers and sisters. These are the things that teach us, grow us and make us strong if we stay the course. These things quietly build a firm foundation under us so we can "take part in everything bright and beautiful that he has for us."

Here are a couple of verses that have kept me motivated and helped me get through the everyday times when I needed God's promises to keep me moving forward on my journey:

> **"So do not throw away your confidence; it will be richly rewarded. You need to persevere so that when you have done the will of God, you will receive what he has promised."** Hebrews 10:35-36 (NIV)

> **"Being confident of this, that he who began a good work in you will carry it on to completion until the day of Christ Jesus."** Philippians 1:6 (NIV)

Trust him and he will move you forward.

Bill has entered a beautiful season in his life. He can take all the years of life and ministerial experience—including the mistakes, setbacks, challenges, victories and miracles—and help people and other rescue missions and recovery ministries in their journeys toward excellence.

He is in a season of imparting blessing and wisdom, and it is beautiful to behold. I have always gleaned from his wisdom and, as a result, I am challenged and sharpened by him daily. We all need someone to help sharpen our minds, and provoke us to be better men, women, wives, mothers, friends, siblings, leaders. In turn, we have the responsibility to seek out those we can encourage, sharpen, challenge and mentor to help them be their very best.

An acorn becomes a mighty oak tree by digging its roots deep; it is shaped by the seasons of life. Bill has been shaped by the mistakes and storms of his life, including the addiction he overcame through Christ. His roots are deep in the foundation of his faith in the Lord.

I believe Bill's best years are still ahead of him. He looks forward to using the experiences that have shaped him as a leader to help guide others in leadership. He has always said, "What God by his grace gave us so freely as we pioneered this ministry, I will share, too." I am proud of the fearless, visionary leader I have the privilege to call my husband. He will be the first to say he is nothing without the grace of his Lord, Jesus Christ.

*Recently, someone asked me about Bill's future. "How can life get any better after you have been in your Promised Land?" I believe the answer is in Bill's favorite verse: "**Now to him who is able to do immeasurably more than all we ask or imagine, according to his power that is at work within us, to him be glory in the church and in Christ Jesus throughout all generations, for ever and ever! Amen.**" Ephesians 3:20-21 (NIV)*

I thank God for the man who never let go of the vision God imparted to him. I know the thousands of program participants and families who now live in freedom from addiction are deeply thankful to him. And we, his family, now have this amazing legacy of faith, compassion and love to embrace. As for me, I am humbled and grateful the Lord allowed me to take part in this great adventure with my faith-filled, fearless visionary leader and beloved husband, Bill Heintz.

Thank you, God, that you saw potential in us to lead your hurting children to freedom. You took a chance on us and by your grace we have done the best we could with what you put in our hands. May those who have been set free in turn see their potential and pay it forward to the glory of God. Amen.

Michele

Living from the Promised Land

It has been two decades since Michele and I made that tearful trip to Bessemer to accept the position of executive director of what is now The Foundry Ministries. I have never gotten weary of living in my Promised Land—watching it grow, praying with men and women determined to make their own journeys of recovery, adding incredibly talented coworkers to the staff, seeing the positive impact we've made on the community of Bessemer.

I have turned in my badge, and my signature on emails and letters is no longer followed with "executive director." That badge now belongs to someone else. I have moved out of my chair and passed along my responsibilities as the leader of this amazing ministry, which I am proud to say has become my Promised Land. But I'm not leaving by a long shot.

When I said "YES, Lord" to the vision of ministering to the addicted, the lost, the hurting, it wasn't attached to a building or a title. As I have moved into my new position as senior pastor and chief spiritual growth officer of The Foundry Ministries, I am still right where I belong—firmly planted in this Promised Land of mine.

And I'm ready for the next part of my "YES" journey.

And what about you? Are you ready for your own road ahead? Are you ready to say "YES, Lord" to whatever his vision for your life might be?

We all have opportunities to lead whether we call ourselves leaders or not. We all have the ability to influence at least one person or a whole circle of people toward success or to their detriment. So no matter who you are, you can choose to make a positive impact or a negative impact on others.

When you lead intentionally and responsibly in the life the Lord has called you to, you make a positive influence on those around you. You have the opportunity to help others as they face their own defining moments in life, overcoming barriers, pushing past the potholes and climbing mountains they never thought they could climb.

Whether you are a mom, dad, teacher, pastor or business owner, you first lead with your attitude. Nobody is perfect and nobody has perfect days, but if you start your day offering your abilities and your shortcomings to God, he will use you in ways far beyond yourself to help your fellow man.

Just as God instructed Moses to use what was "in his hand" to set Israel free from bondage, allow him to use the abilities he has given you to

speak the truth, teach a skill, love the unlovable or offer a job to someone who needs a second chance. Perhaps you might even help someone begin the journey to his or her personal Promised Land!

I promise you, when you give all of your little, God will turn it into more than you can ever imagine.

If there is one thing you take away from this book, make it this:

Do whatever it takes to find God's purpose for your life and then say "YES, Lord." Allow him to help you identify your personal Promised Land. Depend on him to help you reach that incredible place with the guidance of those he brings into your life to accomplish what you can't accomplish on your own.

Let the stick in your hand become the "staff of God" because, when you do, you will go places you never thought you could go. You will do things you never thought you could do. What God wants to do in your life, you cannot even comprehend!

And now, my prayer for you is the prayer from Ephesians 3:16-21 (NIV):

> **I pray that out of his glorious riches he may strengthen you with power through his Spirit in your inner being, so that Christ may dwell in your hearts through faith.**

And I pray that you, being rooted and established in love, may have power, together with all the Lord's holy people, to grasp how wide and long and high and deep is the love of Christ, and to know this love that surpasses knowledge—that you may be filled to the measure of all the fullness of God.

Now to him who is able to do immeasurably more than all we ask or imagine, according to his power that is at work within us, to him be glory in the church and in Christ Jesus throughout all generations, for ever and ever!

Amen.

Share Your YES Journey

Sharing the journey and being part of lives reshaped by the hand of God brings me an enormous amount of joy in my Promised Land.

We would love to share in your YES Journey, as God reshapes your life and moves you into and through your personal Promised Land. Please go to TheYESJourney.org and get your bonus materials, take a look at photos showing our lives throughout our journey (the hairstyles alone will be worth your time), share your detours, potholes, mountains and valleys with us.

The YES Journey Daily Steps

As I've explained throughout this book about my YES Journey to, and in, my personal Promised Land, relying on God's word and faithfulness has been THE sustaining factor for me, and for my family, many days—and sometimes to just get me through the next hour!

To further equip you on your own YES Journey, "The YES Journey Daily Steps" offers encouragement and inspiration through a 90-day devotional guide. It is our hope and prayer that it will give you strength and help you move forward every step and every day.

Here is a full week to get you started:

Monday

Verse: Many are the plans in a man's heart but it is the Lord's purpose that prevails. ~ Proverbs 19:21 (NIV)

Prayer Focus: The Lord's purpose for your life

For Today's Walk: Surrender your plans to the Lord and trust that his purpose will prevail in your life. This is a huge step in your YES Journey! It will help line up your dream with his purpose for you—and his purposes are always the best for us.

Tuesday

Verse: Trust God from the bottom of your heart; don't try to figure out everything on your own. Listen for God's voice in everything you do, everywhere you go; he's the one who will keep you on track. ~ Proverbs 3:5-6 (The Message)

Prayer Focus: Listening for God's voice

For Today's Walk: Now that you are saying "YES" to God's purpose for your life, don't tell him: "Hey, God, thanks for the plan—I've got it from here." He will guide you and move you forward (even when it feels backward) and he will keep you on track.

Wednesday

Verse: "I know the plans I have for you," declares the Lord, "plans to prosper you and not to harm you, plans to give you hope and a future." ~ Jeremiah 29:11 (NIV)

Prayer Focus: Trust and hope in the Lord's plans

For Today's Walk: What are God's plans for you? He certainly did not give Michele and me a map with every place we would go or a script for every thing we would deal with when we started out. If he had, it might have scared us off. But he knew the plan was to grow us and teach us on

our YES Journey so we would be better equipped to live in this Promised Land he planned. His plan worked great for us. Be confident it will for you, too.

Thursday

Verse: I strive always to keep my conscience clear before God and man. ~ Acts 24:16 (NIV)

Prayer Focus: Forgiveness

For Today's Walk: Doing what is right, to keep your conscience clear before God and before people, can be tough—like forgiving and dealing wisely with change and being kind to people who are not kind to you. But a clear conscience will keep you from stumbling over yourself on your YES Journey.

Friday

Verse: Humble yourselves, therefore, under God's mighty hand, that he may lift you up in due time. Cast all your anxiety on him because he cares for you. ~ I Peter 5:6-7 (NIV)

Prayer Focus: Humility before God

For Today's Walk: Giving God your concerns and understanding that he will lift you up when you feel down is an important milestone for

you in your YES Journey. Today, make a list on a sheet of paper of your concerns. Fold up the list as a symbol of giving it to him. Let him work in these areas as you trust that he is with you on the journey, every step of the way.

Saturday

Verse: Brothers and sisters, I do not consider myself yet to have taken hold of it. But one thing I do: Forgetting what is behind and straining toward what is ahead, I press on toward the goal to win the prize for which God has called me heavenward in Christ Jesus. ~ Philippians 3:13-14 (NIV)

Prayer Focus: Moving forward

For Today's Walk: Keep looking forward! As you move forward on your YES Journey, realize that your Promised Land will not look like your past. (It's not supposed to!) You will walk through experiences that are completely different and uncomfortable, but press on and win that personal Promised Land prize the Lord has for you!

Sunday

Verse: The Lord had said to Abram, "Go from your country, your people and your father's household to the land I will show you. I will make you into a great nation, and I will bless you; I will make your name great, and you will be a blessing. I will bless those who bless you, and whoever

curses you I will curse; and all peoples on earth will be blessed through you." So Abram went, as the Lord had told him and Lot went with him.

~ Genesis 12:1-4 (NIV)

Prayer Focus: Obedience

For Today's Walk: Abram didn't know where the Lord was taking him. I didn't know where the Lord was taking me. But he blessed Abram and he has certainly blessed me! If he will do it for us, he will do it for you! So, be obedient, even when it feels like you are leaving everything familiar to get to your personal Promised Land and live your God-given purpose.

Get your copy of "The YES Journey Daily Steps" now at TheYESJour-ney.org. (It's undated so you can start using it the day you receive it and re-use it as often as you would like.)

The YES Journey Study Guide

"The YES Journey Study Guide" takes you on an in-depth walk through many of the Bible verses that helped shape the trials of my YES Journey into triumphs. If you'd like to go deeper, and apply the principles and promises shared in "The YES Journey" book, here is a sample of what you can expect when you order "The YES Journey Study Guide":

"THAT Moment"

God's word is full of "THAT moments." I describe a "THAT moment" as: that point in time when a word, an action, a circumstance knocks you in the head and heart, and directs your steps toward a lifelong calling. A defining moment might tell you something you need to know about yourself. It might tell you to stop what you are doing and start something new. It can scare or exhilarate you—maybe both at the same time! And if it really is a "THAT moment" then you know it is the voice of God.

Read the following verses and use the space provided to answer the following questions:

Genesis 12:1-5

Esther 4:11-5:1

Matthew 4:18-22

Who experienced a "THAT moment" in the verses?

In Genesis:

In Esther:

In Matthew:

Briefly describe the "THAT moment" experience in the verses

In Genesis:

In Esther:

In Matthew:

What changed in his or her life afterward?

In Genesis:

In Esther:

In Matthew:

Have you experienced any "THAT moments" in your life? If you have, briefly describe them below.

What changed in your life afterward? How did you think differently?

How did you act differently?

In the "THAT Moment" section of the book, Bill says:

"He has made you to be somebody, somebody with the purpose, passion and potential to enter into a Promised Land of your own." Do you believe that is true?

Why or why not?

Bill believed the Lord was calling him into full-time ministry, even as a new Christian. Many people are called for specific purposes that do not involve full-time ministry. Esther is a great example and we read her story in Esther 4:11-5:1.

What do you believe the Lord is calling you to do?

Why do you believe that?

If you don't know what he is calling you to do, ask him to show you. Take a few moments and ask him to make his calling clear to you.

Write down what you believe your personal Promised Land might be or look like.

To learn more on your own, with your family or with a small group, order the complete "The YES Journey Study Guide" at TheYESJourney.org

Meet the Authors

Bill Heintz

Bill operated as a "functional addict" without purpose and, as he says, "on a path to nowhere" for many years until a relationship with Jesus Christ changed his heart, his priorities and his life.

As a licensed and ordained minister, he joined The Foundry Ministries (then known as the Bessemer Rescue Mission) in 1996 and led the organization as executive director for 20 years, realizing his vision of offering men and women caught in the grip of addiction the tools to permanently transform their lives. Before coming to The Foundry, he served as associate pastor at Calvary Assembly in Decatur, Alabama, and then as interim director for the Downtown Rescue Mission in Huntsville.

Michele Heintz

Michele has been influential in women's ministries since 1984, previously pioneering programs in local churches in Alabama and Tennessee.

Since coming to The Foundry Ministries in 1996 with her husband, Rev. Bill Heintz, she has served in many capacities including director of administration, assistant director and senior director of women's programs, through which she led the growth of the Women's Recovery Program and the restructuring of the Rescue Program.

Michele and Bill have five children, nine grandchildren and three great grandchildren and live near Birmingham, Alabama.

Julie Larocco

Julie grew up around a rescue mission, which her grandparents founded and her parents operated. She says it was a strange world to grow up in but one she wouldn't trade. She later consulted with missions around the country before she began serving as chief development officer at Kansas City Rescue Mission in 2009.

Someone recommended Bill and Michele contact her to help them with basic fundraising and public relations not long after they moved to The Foundry Ministries in 1996. The three are now like family, even though they are physically many miles apart.

Julie and her husband Rob live in Kansas City. Her three children and 10 grandchildren all live close by.